CBSE Term II
2022

Political Science
Class XII

- Complete Theory Covering NCERT
- Cased Based Questions
- Short/Long Answer Questions
- 3 Practice Papers

Author
Priyanshi Verma

arihant
ARIHANT PRAKASHAN (School Division Series)

ARIHANT PRAKASHAN (School Division Series)

卐 **Administrative & Production Offices**

Regd. Office

'Ramchhaya' 4577/15, Agarwal Road, Darya Ganj, New Delhi -110002
Tele: 011- 47630600, 43518550

卐 **Head Office**

Kalindi, TP Nagar, Meerut (UP) - 250002, Tel: 0121-7156203, 7156204

卐 **Sales & Support Offices**

Agra, Ahmedabad, Bengaluru, Bareilly, Chennai, Delhi, Guwahati, Hyderabad, Jaipur, Jhansi, Kolkata, Lucknow, Nagpur & Pune.

卐 **ISBN :** 978-93-25796-98-0

PO No : TXT-XX-XXXXXXX-X-XX

Published by Arihant Publications (India) Ltd.

For further information about the books published by Arihant, log on to www.arihantbooks.com or e-mail at info@arihantbooks.com

Follow us on    

Contents

Syllabus

CBSE Term II Class XII

Units	Contents	Weightage (in Marks)
PART A: CONTEMPORARY WORLD POLITICS		
1.	New Centers of Power	08
2.	South Asia and the Contemporary World	06
3.	Globalization	06
PART B: POLITICS IN INDIA SINCE INDEPENDENCE		
1.	Parties and the Party Systems in India	06
2.	Democratic Resurgence	06
3.	Indian Politics: Trends and Developments	08
Total		**40**

CBSE Circular

Acad - 51/2021, 05 July 2021

Exam Scheme Term I & II

केन्द्रीय माध्यमिक शिक्षा बोर्ड

(शिक्षा मंत्रालय, भारत सरकार के अधीन एक स्वायत संगठन)

CENTRAL BOARD OF SECONDARY EDUCATION

(An Autonomous Organisation under the Ministryof Education, Govt. of India)

CBSE/DIR (ACAD)/2021

Date: July 05, 2021
Circular No: Acad-51/2021

All the Heads of Schools affiliated to CBSE

Subject: Special Scheme of Assessment for Board Examination Classes X and XII for the Session 2021-22

COVID 19 pandemic caused almost all CBSE schools to function in a virtual mode for most part of the academic session of 2020-21. Due to the extreme risk associated with the conduct of Board examinations during the second wave in April 2021, CBSE had to cancel both its class X and XII Board examinations of the year 2021 and results are to be declared on the basis of a credible, reliable, flexible and valid alternative assessment policy. This, in turn, also necessitated deliberations over alternative ways to look at the learning objectives as well as the conduct of the Board Examinations for the academic session 2021-22 in case the situation remains unfeasible.

CBSE has also held stake holder consultations with Government schools as well as private independent schools from across the country especially schools from the remote rural areas and a majority of them have requested for the rationalization of the syllabus, similar to last year in view of reduced time permitted for organizing online classes. The Board has also considered the concerns regarding differential availability of electronic gadgets, connectivity and effectiveness of online teaching and other socio-economic issues specially with respect to students from economically weaker section and those residing in far flung areas of the country. In a survey conducted by CBSE, it was revealed that the rationalized syllabus notified for the session 2020-21 was effective for schools in covering the syllabus and helped learners in achieving learning objectives in a less stressful manner.

In the above backdrop and in line with the Board's continued focus on assessing stipulated learning outcomes by making the examinations competencies and core concepts based, student-centric, transparent, technology-driven, and having advance provision of alternatives for different future scenarios, the following schemes are introduced for the Academic Session for Class X and Class XII 2021-22.

केन्द्रीय माध्यमिक शिक्षा बोर्ड

(शिक्षा मंत्रालय, भारत सरकार के अधीन एक स्वायत संगठन)

CENTRAL BOARD OF SECONDARY EDUCATION

(An Autonomous Organisation under the Ministryof Education, Govt. of India)

Special Scheme for 2021-22

A. Academic session to be divided into 2 Terms with approximately 50% syllabus in each term:

The syllabus for the Academic session 2021-22 will be divided into 2 terms by following a systematic approach by looking into the interconnectivity of concepts and topics by the Subject Experts and the Board will conduct examinations at the end of each term on the basis of the bifurcated syllabus. This is done to increase the probability of having a Board conducted classes X and XII examinations at the end of the academic session.

B. The syllabus for the Board examination 2021-22 will be rationalized similar to that of the last academic session to be notified in July 2021. For academic transactions, however, schools will follow the curriculum and syllabus released by the Board vide Circular no. F.1001/CBSE-Acad/Curriculum/2021 dated 31 March 2021. Schools will also use alternative academic calendar and inputs from the NCERT on transacting the curriculum.

C. Efforts will be made to make Internal Assessment/ Practical/ Project work more credible and valid as per the guidelines and Moderation Policy to be announced by the Board to ensure fair distribution of marks.

Details of Curriculum Transaction

- Schools will continue teaching in distance mode till the authorities permit in-person mode of teaching in schools.

- **Classes IX-X: Internal Assessment** (throughout the year-irrespective of Term I and II) would include the *3 periodic tests, student enrichment, portfolio and practical work/ speaking listening activities/ project.*

- **Classes XI-XII: Internal Assessment** (throughout the year-irrespective of Term I and II) would include end of topic or unit tests/ exploratory activities/ practicals/ projects.

- Schools would create a student profile for all assessment undertaken over the year and retain the evidences in digital format.

- CBSE will facilitate schools to upload marks of Internal Assessment on the CBSE IT platform.

- Guidelines for Internal Assessment for all subjects will also be released along with the rationalized term wise divided syllabus for the session 2021-22.The Board would also provide additional resources like sample assessments, question banks, teacher training etc. for more reliable and valid internal assessments.

Term I Examinations:

- At the end of the first term, the Board will organize **Term I Examination** in a flexible schedule to be conducted between November-December 2021 with a window period of 4-8 weeks for schools situated in different parts of country and abroad. Dates for conduct of examinations will be notified subsequently.

- The Question Paper will have Multiple Choice Questions (MCQ) including case-based MCQs and MCQs on assertion-reasoning type. Duration of test will be **90 minutes** and it will cover only the rationalized syllabus of **Term I only** (i.e. approx. 50% of the entire syllabus).

- Question Papers will be sent by the CBSE to schools along with marking scheme.

- The exams will be conducted under the supervision of the External Center Superintendents and Observers appointed by CBSE.

- The responses of students will be captured on OMR sheets which, after scanning may be directly uploaded at CBSE portal or alternatively may be evaluated and marks obtained will be uploaded by the school on the very same day. The final direction in this regard will be conveyed to schools by the Examination Unit of the Board.

- Marks of the **Term I** Examination will contribute to the final overall score of students.

Term II Examination/ Year-end Examination:

- At the end of the second term, the Board would organize **Term II or Year-end Examination** based on the rationalized syllabus of Term II only (i.e. approximately 50% of the entire syllabus).

- This examination would be held around **March-April 2022** at the examination centres fixed by the Board.

- The paper will be of **2 hours duration** and have questions of different formats (case-based/ situation based, open ended- short answer/ long answer type).

- In case the situation is not conducive for normal descriptive examination **a 90 minute MCQ based exam** will be conducted at the end of the Term II also.

- Marks of the Term II Examination would contribute to the final overall score.

केन्द्रीय माध्यमिक शिक्षा बोर्ड

(शिक्षा मंत्रालय, भारत सरकार के अधीन एक स्वायत संगठन)

CENTRAL BOARD OF SECONDARY EDUCATION

(An Autonomous Organisation under the Ministryof Education, Govt. of India)

<u>Assessment / Examination as per different situations</u>

A. In case the situation of the pandemic improves and students are able to come to schools or centres for taking the exams.

Board would conduct Term I and Term II examinations at schools/centres and the theory marks will be distributed equally between the two exams.

B. In case the situation of the pandemic forces complete closure of schools during November-December 2021, but Term II exams are held at schools or centres.

Term I MCQ based examination would be done by students online/offline from home - in this case, the weightage of this exam for the final score would be reduced, and weightage of Term II exams will be increased for declaration of final result.

C. In case the situation of the pandemic forces complete closure of schools during March-April 2022, but Term I exams are held at schools or centres.

Results would be based on the performance of students on Term I MCQ based examination and internal assessments. The weightage of marks of Term I examination conducted by the Board will be increased to provide year end results of candidates.

D. In case the situation of the pandemic forces complete closure of schools and Board conducted Term I and II exams are taken by the candidates from home in the session 2021-22.

Results would be computed on the basis of the Internal Assessment/Practical/Project Work and Theory marks of Term-I and II exams taken by the candidate from home in Class X / XII subject to the moderation or other measures to ensure validity and reliability of the assessment.

In all the above cases, data analysis of marks of students will be undertaken to ensure the integrity of internal assessments and home based exams.

Dr. Joseph Emmanuel
Director (Academics)

PART A

Contemporary World Politics

1. New Centres of Power
2. South Asia and the Contemporary World
3. Globalisation

CHAPTER 01

New Centers of Power

In this Chapter...

- European Union (EU)
- Association of South-East Asian Nations (ASEAN)
- South Asian Association for Regional Cooperation (SAARC)
- BRICS
- Nations : Russia, India, Israel and China

With the end of bipolarity in the world politics, it became evident that new centres of economic and political power could limit the powers of US dominance. The New Centres of Power emerged in the form of European Union (Europe), the Association of South East Asian Nations (ASEAN) in Asia, SAARC, BRICS in different parts of the world.

These organisations tried to transform the countries in the region into prosperous economies. On the other hand, rise of China's economy has also made a great impact on the world politics.

European Union (EU)

After the end of the Second World War in 1945, there was a dilemma among many European leaders over the status of Europe. The Second World War destroyed many of the assumptions and structures on which European states had based their relations. The Cold War aided the integration of Europe after 1945. The European economy was revived by financial support provided by USA under the 'Marshall Plan'. A new collective security structure under NATO was created by the US.

Under the **Marshall Plan**[1], the **Organisation for European Economic Cooperation** (OEEC) was established in 1948. It acts like a mechanism to aid the West European states. Another step in the direction of political cooperation was the establishment of the **Council of Europe** in **1949**.

Gradually, the process of economic integration of European capitalist countries proceeded leading to the formation of **European Economic Community** in 1957. This process acquired a political dimension with the foundation of the European Parliament. The collapse of Soviet Bloc led to the establishment of the European Union (EU) in 1992. The **European Union** was formally established on **1st November, 1993**.

EU was founded for a common foreign and security policy, cooperation on justice and home affairs, and the creation of a single currency.

Although it doesn't have its own constitution but it comprises of its own flag, anthem, founding date and currency. It also has some form of common foreign and security policy in dealing with other nations. EU's area of cooperation was expanded while acquiring new members especially from the erstwhile Soviet bloc. The EU has economic, political and diplomatic and military influence.

---

1. **Marshall Plan** A plan introduced by USA to provide financial help for the revival of European economy.

Economic Influence of EU

The economic influence of European Union is discussed below

- EU is the world's second biggest economy with a GDP of more than \$17 trillion in 2016, next to the United States of America.
- Its currency Euro can pose a threat to the dominance of US dollar. EU's share of world trade is much larger than that of US.
- It has an economic influence over its closest neighbours as well as in Asia and Africa.
- It also functions as an important bloc in international economic organisations such as WTO.

Political and Diplomatic Influence of EU

The political and diplomatic influence of EU is discussed below

- One member of EU France, holds permanent seat in the UN Security Council with several non-permanent members.
- The EU is enabled to influence some US policies such as the current US position on Iran's Nuclear Programme.
- Its diplomacy, economic investments and negotiations have been effective with China particularly on issues of human rights and environmental degradation.

Military Influence of EU

The military influence of EU is discussed below

- EU's combined armed forces are the second largest in the world and comes second after US in defence expenditure.
- Britain and France as EU members also possess nuclear arsenal of 550 nuclear warheads. It is also the world's second most important source of space and communication technology.
- EU is able to intervene in economic, political and social areas. But in many areas member states have their own foreign and defence policies that are often at odds with each other. For instance, Britain was by the side of US during the Iraq invasion whereas Germany and France oppose the American policy.
- **Euro- skepticism** [2] is evident in some parts of Europe about the Europe's integrationist agenda. For instance, UK's former PM Margaret Thatcher kept UK out of the European market. Denmark and Sweden resisted Maastricht Treaty and the adoption of Euro. Thus, it limits the ability of EU to act in matters of foreign relations and defence.

Association of South-East Asian Nations (ASEAN)

Association of South-East Asian Nations (ASEAN) was established in 1967 with the signing of the ASEAN declaration (Bangkok Declaration) by its founding countries. The founding members of ASEAN are Indonesia, Malaysia, Philippines, Singapore and Thailand.

Over the years, Brunei Darussalam, Vietnam, Lao PDR, Myanmar (Burma) and Cambodia also joined ASEAN taking its strength to ten members.

Therefore, ASEAN is a regional organisation which was established to promote political and social stability amid rising tensions among the Asia-Pacific's post colonial states. The motto of ASEAN is **One Vision, One Identity, One Community**.

Background of ASEAN

This Asian region faced the economic and political consequences of numerous colonialisms, both European and Japanese, before and during Second World War. It faced issues of nation-building, poverty and economic backwardness, and the pressure to align with one of the great powers during the Cold War at the end of the war.

Efforts to unite Asia and the Third World, such as the **Bandung Conference** and the **Non-Aligned Movement**, were unsuccessful in establishing informal cooperation and interaction conventions. As a result, the Southeast Asian alternative by establishing the Association of South East Asian Nations (ASEAN).

In the year 1995, the members of ASEAN signed a deal to create a nuclear free zone in South-East Asia. The ASEAN adopted **Vision 2020** in 1997 and by 2015 it launched ASEAN **Community** which comprised of these pillars.

- ASEAN Political -Security Community
- ASEAN Economy Community
- ASEAN Socio-cultural Community

Objectives of ASEAN

The objectives of ASEAN are as follows

- To accelerate economic growth, social progress and cultural development for properous and peaceful community of South-East Asian Nations.
- To promote regional peace and stability through abiding respect for justice and the rule of law.
- To promote active collaboration and mutual assistance on matters of common interests in the economic, social, cultural, technical scientific and administrative fields.
- To create a common market and production base within the ASEAN states and aid social and economic development.

---

2. **Euro- skepticism** It refers to a European political doctrine that advocates disengagement from the European Union (EU).

ASEAN Socio-Cultural Community

The ASEAN Socio-Cultural Community is all about realising the full potential of ASEAN citizens. It is working towards the following aims

- A committed, participative and socially responsible community for the benefit of ASEAN people.
- A sustainable community that promotes social development and environmental protection.
- An inclusive community that promotes high quality of life, equitable access to opportunities for all and promotes and protects human rights, etc.

ASEAN Security Community

The ASEAN Security Community was based on the notion to avoid territorial disputes, so that it would not develop into armed confrontation. For this, ASEAN had several agreements into force by which member states promised to uphold peace, neutrality, cooperation, non-interference and respect for national differences and sovereign rights. **ASEAN Regional Forum** (ARF) was established in 1994 to carry out coordination of security and foreign policy.

ASEAN Economic Community

ASEAN is principally an economic association, while the ASEAN region is much smaller economy than US, the EU and Japan's economy is growing much faster. The objectives of ASEAN Economic Community are

- To create a common market and production base within ASEAN states to aid social and economic development in the region.
- To improve the existing ASEAN Dispute Settlement Mechanism for resolving economic dispute.
- To create a **Free Trade Agreement** (FTA) for investment, labour and services.

ASEAN Vision 2020

ASEAN is rapidly growing into an important regional organisation with its Vision 2020, to define an outward-looking role for ASEAN in international community. It is build upon its existing policy to encourage negotiations over conflicts in the region. Thus, ASEAN had mediated the end of the Cambodian conflict, East Timor crisis and meets annually to discuss East Asian cooperation.

The current economic strength of ASEAN is especially its economic relevance as a trading and investment partner to the growing Asian economies such as India and China, makes this an attractive proposition. India's foreign policy did not gave much attention to ASEAN during Cold War years, but in recent times, it has tried to amend it and have signed **FTA's** with three ASEAN members, **Singapore, Thailand** and **Malaysia.**

However, ASEAN's strength lies in its policies of **interaction** and **consultation** with member states, with discussion partners and with other non-regional organisation. Further, it is the only regional association to provide political forum for Asia and other major powers to discuss political and security concerns.

South Asian Association for Regional Cooperation (SAARC)

The South Asian Association for Regional Cooperation was established with the signing the **SAARC charter** in Dhaka on 8th December, 1985. It was a major regional initiative by the South Asian States to evolve cooperation through multilateral means.

The idea of regional cooperation in South Asia was raised in November 1980. After consultations, the foreign secretaries of the seven founding countries Bangladesh, Bhutan, India, Maldives, Nepal, Pakistan and Sri Lanka met for the first time in Colombo in April 1981.

The headquarters and secretariat of the association are at Kathmandu, Nepal. Afghanistan became the newest member of SAARC at the 13th annual summit in 2005.

There are currently nine observers to SAARC namely

- Australia
- China
- The European Union
- Iran
- Japan
- The Republic of Korea
- Mauritius
- Myanmar
- The United States of America

Objectives of SAARC

The objectives of SAARC are as follows

- To promote the welfare of the people of South Asia and to improve their quality of life.
- To accelerate economic growth, social progress and cultural development in the region and to provide all individuals the opportunity to live in dignity and to realise their full potential.
- To promote and strengthen collective self-reliance among the countries of South Asia.
- To contribute to mutual trust, understanding and appreciation of one another's problem.
- To promote active collaboration and mutual assistance in the economic, social, cultural, technical and scientific fields.
- To strengthen cooperation with other developing countries.
- To strengthen cooperation among themselves in international forums on matters of common interests.
- To cooperate with international and regional organisations with similar aims and purposes.

SAARC and its Importance

SAARC comprises 3% of the world's area, 21% of the world's population and 3.8% of the global economy.

- **Creating Synergies** It is the world's most densely populated region and one of the most fertile areas. SAARC countries have common tradition, dress, food and culture and political aspects thereby synergising their actions. SAARC has initiated **SAFTA** to free trade zones for whole South Asia for collective economic activity.
- **Common Solutions** All SAARC countries have common problems and issues like poverty, illiteracy, malnutrition, natural disasters, internal conflicts, industrial and technological backwardness, low GDP and poor socio-economic condition.
- These countries uplift their living standards thereby creating common areas of development and progress having common solutions.

Significance of SAARC for India

The significance of SAARC for India is disscussed below

- **Economic Integration** India's **Look East Policy** links South Asian economies with South-East Asia will bring further economic intergration and prosperity to India mainly in the Service sector.
- **Geostrategic Significance** It can counter China through engaging Nepal, Bhutan, the Maldives and Sri Lanka in development process and economic cooperation.
- **Regional Stability** SAARC can help in creation of mutual trust and peace within the region.
- **Global Leadership Role** It offers India a platform to showcase its leadership in the region by taking up extra responsibilities.

Limitations of SAARC

The limitations of SAARC are disscussed below

- SAARC is growing at a slow pace due to the political differences among its member states.
- Conflicts between India and Pakistan led to bilateral issues like Kashmir issue.
- India's neighbours feared that India intends to dominate them by influencing at the political and societal level.
- SAARC members in majority belong to developing or least developing countries which creates insufficiency of funds.

BRICS

BRICS is an acronym for five emerging economies of the world – **Brazil, Russia, India, China, South Africa**. The term BRIC was coined by Jim O' Neil, the then Chairman of Goldman Sachs in 2001. BRIC was founded in 2006 in Russia. BRIC turned into BRICS after the inclusion of South Africa in its first meeting in the year 2009.

The key objectives of BRICS are primarily to cooperate and distribute mutual economic benefits among its members besides non-interference in the internal polices of each nation and mutual equality. The 12th conference of BRICS was concluded in Russia in 2020. It was chaired by Russian President Vladimir Putin. The 13th Conference of BRICS was held in India in June 2021 under the Chairmanship of India's Prime Minister Shri Narendra Modi.

Structure of BRICS

The structure of BRICS comprises of

- BRICS does not exist in the form of organisation, but it is an annual summit between the supreme leaders of five nations.
- The Chairmanship of the forum is rotated annually among the members in accordance with the acronym B-R-I-C-S.
- BRICS cooperation in the past decade has expanded to include an annual programme of over 100 sectoral meetings.

Objectives of BRICS

The objective of the BRICS can be summarised below

- The BRICS seeks to deepen, broaden and intensify cooperation within the grouping and among the individual countries for more sustainable, equitable and mutually beneficial development.
- BRICS takes into consideration each members growth, development and poverty objectives to ensure that relations are built on the respective country's economic strength and to avoid competition where possible.
- To enhance and diversify trade and investment cooperation that support value addition among the BRICS countries.
- To enhance market access opportunities and facilitate market interlinkages.
- To seek funther interaction and cooperation with non-BRICS countries and international organisations and forums.
- BRICS is emerging as a new and promising political-diplomatic entity with diverse objectives, far beyond the original objective of reforming global financial institutions.

Importance of BRICS for India

- India can benefit from collective strength of BRICS by way of **consultation** and **cooperation** as well as topical global issues, such as international terrorism, climate change, food and energy security, reforms of global governance institutions etc.
- India remains engaged with the other BRICS countries on its NSG membership.

- The **New Development Bank** (NDB) will help India to raise and avail resources for their infrastructure and sustainable development projects. The NDB has approved its first set of loans, which included a loan of US $ 250 million in respect of India for Multitranche Financing Facility for Renewable Energy Financing Scheme.

Nations : Russia, India, Isreal and China

After the disintegration of Soviet Union, some of the nations emerged as Global power in 21st century. For example, Russia emerged as a strong successor of USSR, India and Israel emerged as powerful and important nations in 21st century and China can be seen as strong emerging Economic power since 1978.

Russia

Even before the disintegration of Soviet Union, Russia has been its largest part. Russia emerged as the strong successor of USSR (Union of Soviet Socialist Republic), after the dissolution of the Soviet Union in late 1980's and the early 1990's. Russia has emerged as one of the powerful country in the global world as it has vast reserves of nature resources, minerals and gases. In addition, Russia is a nuclear state with a huge stock of sophisticated weapons. It is also a permanent member of the UN Security Council, called **P-5**.

Economic Model of Russia

Russia's economy is a mixed and transitional economy of upper-middle income, with vast natural resources, particularly oil and natural gas. Russia's GDP is currently at eleventh position in the world.

India

India has emerged as an important global power in the 21st century. The world is experiencing the power and rise of India in a multidimensional way. With the population of 135 crores the economic, cultural, strategic position of the country is very strong.

Economic Model of India

From an economic perspective, targeting the goal of a $ 5 trillion economy 2024-25, a competitive huge market, an ancient inclusive culture with 200 million people of Indian Diaspora spreading across the globe impart distinct meaning and salience to India as a new centre of power in 21st century.

The military of India is self sufficient with indigenous nuclear technology making it another nuclear power from a strategic perspective. Projects like **Make in India** sets

another milestone in India economy. Therefore, all these changes are making India an important power in the present world.

Israel

Israel has also emerged as one of the most powerful nations in the 21st century in terms of science and technology, defence and intelligence. Israel has reached to the new heights of global political standing by virtue of its strong defence prowess, technological innovations, industrilisation and agricultural development.

Israel being a small Jewish-Zionist nation is placed in the contemporary global politics in general and the Arab-dominated West Asian politics in particular.

Economic Model of Israel

Israel's economy is a well-developed free-market economy that is technologically advanced. After the United States, it has the world's second-largest number of start-up enterprises. Its top exports include cut diamonds, high-tech equipment, and pharmaceuticals. Crude oil, foodstuffs, raw materials, and military equipment are among the country's main imports.

China

China has been growing as an economic power since 1978. It is estimated to overtake US as the world's largest economy by 2040. It has enormous regional influence due to its economic integration into the region. Factors like population, landmass, resources, regional location and political influence adds to its power along with a strong economy.

Economic Model of China

- Under the leadership of Mao in 1949, the economy of the Communist China was based on the **Soviet model**. At that time China was economically backward and it put an end to its link with the capitalist world. It now relied on its own resources.

- The model was to generate a state-owned heavy industries sector from the capital accumulated from agriculture. Due to the shortage of foreign exchange to buy technology and goods from the world market, China substitute imports by domestic goods.

- This model empowers China to utilise its resources and helped to establish the foundations of an industrial economy. Employment and social welfare was assured to all the citizens. China moved ahead of most developing countries in providing better education and health facilities.

- The economic growth was at a respectable rate but though it was not sufficient to meet the needs of the people. Agriculture sector was unable to generate economic surplus. China was going through similar crises like the USSR i.e. slow pace industrial production and low per capita income.

New Economic Policy of China

- Major policy decisions were taken in the 1970's by the Chinese leadership. China ended its political and economic isolation with US in 1972.
- Premier Zhou Enlai proposed **Four modernisations** i.e. agriculture, industry, science and technology and military in 1973. Later in 1978, Deng Xiaoping announced the **Open door policy**[3] and economic reforms in China.
- Open door policy was to generate higher productivity by investments of capital and technology from abroad. Market economy was adopted and their economy was opened step by step.
- Agriculture sector was privatised in 1982 followed by privatisation of industry in 1998. Trade barriers were eliminated in **Special Economic Zones** (SEZ's) where enterprises were set by the foreign investors.
- State plays a dominant role in setting up a market based economy in China.

Impact of New Economic Policy

The impact of New Economic Policy of China was as follows

- The new economic policies helped the Chinese economy to deal with stagnation.
- Privatisation of agriculture resulted in rise of agricultural production and rural incomes which helped the rural economy growth at a faster pace.
- The new trading laws and creation of Special Economic Zones attracted foreign players and foreign trade.
- China has become an important place for Foreign Direct Investment (FDI) in the world. Now, China has large foreign exchange reserves which allow it to make big investments in other countries. China's accession to the WTO in 2001 also helped its opening to the outside world.
- Although the Chinese economy has improved, still it did not benefit everyone in China. The rate of unemployment has risen, working conditions and female employment is bad. Environmental degradation and corruption has also increased besides these rise in economic inequality between rural and urban residents.

Timeline of European Integration

1951 April	Six west European countries, France, West Germany, Italy, Belgium, the Netherlands and Luxembourg sign the Treaty of Paris establishing the European Coal and Steel Community (ECSC).
1957 March 25	These six countries sign the Treaties of Rome establishing the European Economic Community (EEC) and the European Atomic Energy Community (Euratom).
1973 January	Denmark, Ireland and the United Kingdom join the European Community (EC).
1979 June	First direct elections to the European Parliament.
1981 January	Greece joins the EC.
1985 June	The Schengen Agreement abolishes border controls among the EC members.
1986 January	Spain and Portugal join the EC.
1990 October	Unification of Germany.
1992 February 7	The Treaty of Maastricht was signed establishing the European Union (EU).
1993 January	The single market was created.
1995 January	Austria, Finland and Sweden join the EU.
2002 January	Euro, the new currency, was introduced in the 12 EU members.
2004 May	Ten new members, Cyprus, the Czech Republic, Estonia, Hungary, Latvia, Lithuania, Malta, Poland, Slovakia and Slovenia join the EU.
2007 January	Bulgaria and Romania join the EU. Slovenia adopts the Euro.
2009 December	The Lisbon Treaty came into force.
2012	The EU is awarded the Noble Peace Prize.
2013	Croatia becomes the 28th member of the EU.
2016	Referendum in Britain, 51.9 per cent voters decide that Britain exit (BRE XIT) from the EU. (The United Kingdom left the EU on 31st January, 2020)

---

3. **Open Door Policy** The policy adopted to invite investment of capital and technology from abroad.

Chapter Practice

Objective Questions

• Multiple Choice Questions

1. In which year, the Organisation for European Economic Cooperation was established?
   (a) 1949   (b) 1948
   (c) 1945   (d) 1957

Ans. (b) The Organisation of European Economic Cooperation was established in 1948 to channel aid to the West European states.

2. .... Plan influenced the establishment of the Organisation for European Economic Cooperation in 1948.
   (a) Morgenthau Plan   (b) Maastricht
   (c) NATO   (d) Marshall

Ans. (d) Marshall Plan influenced the establishment of the Organisation for European Economic Cooperation in 1948.

3. Name the countries which resisted Maastricht Treaty.
   (a) Britain and France   (b) France and USA
   (c) Germany and Britain   (d) Denmark and Sweden

Ans. (d) Denmark and Sweden resisted the Maastricht Treaty. The treaty is formally known as the Treaty of Europe responsible for creation of European Union signed in 1991.

4. Which of the following statement(s) is/are correct with regard to the European Union?
   (i) The EU over the time has turned from economic union to a political one.
   (ii) The attempt to EU to have its own constitution failed.
   (iii) It has its own flag, anthem, founding date and currency.
   Codes
   (a) Only (i)   (b) Only (ii)
   (c) Only (iii)   (d) All of these

Ans. (d) Among the given options all are correct. The EU has changed from economic union to a political one. The attempt of EU to have its own constitution failed. It has its own flag, anthem, founding date and currency.

5. Two member countries of European Union are ....
   (a) Japan and China
   (b) Australia and Mauritius
   (c) Poland and Czech Republic
   (d) Indonesia and Malaysia

Ans. (c) Two member countries of European Union are Poland and Czech Republic. The EU is a group of 27 political and economic union countries. The latest country to join EU is Croatia in 2013.

6. Which of the following statements is correct about the ASEAN way?
   (i) Reflects the lifestyle of ASEAN members.
   (ii) A form of interaction among ASEAN members that is informal and cooperative.
   (iii) The defence policy followed by the ASEAN members.
   (iv) The road that connects all the ASEAN members.
   Codes
   (a) Both (i) and (iii)
   (b) Both (ii) and (iv)
   (c) Only (ii)
   (d) Only (iv)

Ans. (c) ASEAN way is a form of interaction among ASEAN members that is informal and cooperative.

7. .... is the organisation of ASEAN that deals with the security.
   (a) ASEAN Economic Community
   (b) ASEAN Socio Community
   (c) ASEAN Security Community
   (d) ASEAN Cultural Community

Ans. (c) ASEAN Security Community is the organisation of ASEAN that deals with the security.

8. Two founder members of ASEAN are .... and ....
   (a) Australia and China
   (b) Indonesia and Malaysia
   (c) Mauritius and Myanmar
   (d) Cambodia and Vietnam

Ans. (b) Two founder member of ASEAN are Indonesia and Malaysia. The other founder member countries are - Philippines, Singapore and Thailand.

9. The ten Stalks of Paddy (Rice) shown in the ASEAN Flag symbolise ....

(a) Unity of ASEAN as it represents ten members of South-East Asian countries.

(b) Disintegration of South -East Asian countries.

(c) Political and Social stability of ASEAN member countries.

(d) None of the above

Ans. (a) The ten Stalks of Paddy (Rice) shown in the ASEAN Flag symbolise unity of ASEAN as it represents ten members of South-East Asian countries.

10. Consider the following and arrange them in correct sequence.

(i) ASEAN Vision

(ii) European Union

(iii) European Economic Community

(iv) Open Door Policy

Codes

(a) (ii), (i), (iv) and (iii)   (b) (iii), (i), (iv) and (ii)

(c) (i), (ii), (iii) and (iv)   (d) (ii), (iv), (i) and (iii)

Ans. (b) European Economic Community—1957

ASEAN Vision—1967

Open Door Policy—1978

European Union—1993

11. Which of the following nations adopted an 'Open Door Policy'?

(a) China   (b) South Korea

(c) Japan   (d) USA

Ans. (a) China adopted an Open Door Policy' Deng Xiaoping announced the Open Door Policy in 1978 for foreign companies to invest and establish in China.

12. China entered into bilateral relations with .... (a major country) in 1972.

(a) USA   (b) Russia   (c) India   (d) Israel

Ans. (a) China entered into bilateral relations with USA in 1972.

13. Which among the following was the first non-communist country to establish an embassy in China?

(a) India   (b) USA   (c) Japan   (d) Russia

Ans. (a) India was the first non-communist country to establish an embassy in China. China and India are two of the major regional powers in Asia and two most populous countries in the world.

14. Consider the following statements about objectives of establishing regional organisations.

(i) To promote regional peace and stability based on rule of law.

(ii) To develop the countries politically so that they can have an impact on the decision-making process at the global level.

(iii) To accelerate economic growth of the native or indigenous forces by establishing cooperation and consensus.

Select the correct statement(s) through following codes.

(a) Both (i) and (iii)   (b) Both (ii) and (iii)

(c) Only (iii)   (d) All of these

Ans. (d) All the statements given above are the objectives of establishing regional organisations.

15. Study the following picture and answer the questions.

What does the fifteen status on ship represent?

(a) Group of South Asian Countries

(b) Group of European Capitalist Countries

(c) Group of Middle East Countries

(d) Group of African Countries

Ans. (b) The fifteen stars on the ship represent a group of fifteen European capitalist countries established in 1992.

16. Study the following picture and answer the questions.

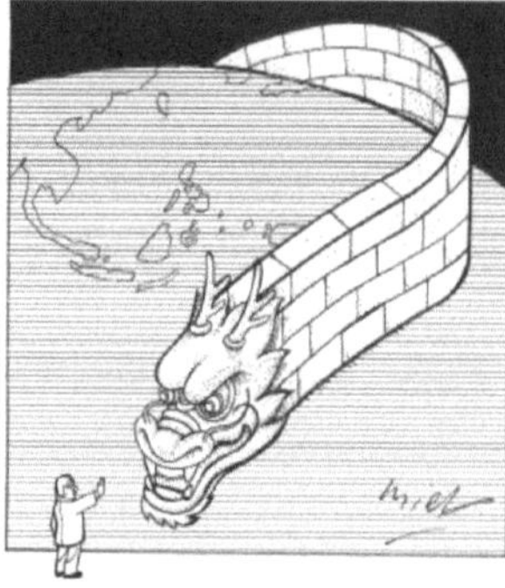

The cartoon depicts the economic rise of which country?

(a) USA   (b) Russia   (c) China   (d) India

Ans. (c) The cartoon depicts the economic rise of China; as China adopted communist ideology.

• Assertion-Reasoning MCQs

Directions (Q. Nos. 17-20) In the question given below, there are two statements marked as Assertion (A) and Reason (R). Read the statements and choose the correct options.

Codes

(a) Both A and R are true and R is the correct explanation of A.

(b) Both A and R are true, but R is not the correct explanation of A.

(c) A is true, but R is false.

(d) A is false, but R is true.

17. Assertion (A) The EU has started to act more as a dictator state.

Reason (R) It also has some form of a common foreign and security policy in its dealings with other nations.

Ans. (d) A is false because the European Union has started to act more as a nation state. R is true as it has some form of a common foreign and security policy in its dealings with other nation. The EU has tried to expand areas of cooperation while acquiring new members.

18. Assertion (A) ASEAN's economy is larger than that of the EU and the US.

Reason (R) ASEAN was and still remains principally an economic association .

Ans. (d) A is false as ASEAN region as a whole is a much smaller economy as compared to the US, EU and Japan.

R is true as ASEAN was and still remains principally an economic association for the growth in its influence both in region and beyond.

19. Assertion (A) ASEAN was develop to pose a military and economic threat to EU.

Reason (R) The objectives of ASEAN were primarily to accelerate economic growth and through that 'social and cultural development.'

Ans. (d) A is false as ASEAN was formed in 1967 by Indonesia, Malaysia, Philippines, Singapore and Thailand to accelerate economic growth and through that social and cultural development.

20. Assertion (A) China had considerable influence and control on the periphery of its borders based on its unique tributary system.

Reason (R) At different times in China's long history of dynastic rule, Mongolia, Korea, parts of Indo-China and Tibet accepted China's authority.

Ans. (a) Both A and R are true and R is the correct explanation of A. China was a great power in Asia before the advent of imperialism. Therefore, China had considerable influence and control on its borders. Mongolia, Korea were parts of Indo-China and Tibet accepted China's authority.

• Case Based MCQs

1. Read the given passage and answer the following questions.

ASEAN was and still remains principally an economic association. While the ASEAN region as a whole is a much smaller economy compared to the US, the EU and Japan, its economy is growing much faster than all these. This accounts for the growth in its influence both in the region and beyond. The objectives of the ASEAN Economic Community are to create a common market and production base within ASEAN states and to aid social and economic development in the region. The Economic Community would also like to improve the existing ASEAN Dispute Settlement Mechanism to resolve economic disputes. ASEAN has focused on creating a Free Trade Area (FTA) for investment, labour and services. The US and China have already moved fast to negotiate FTAs with ASEAN.

(i) How many members are there in ASEAN?
(a) 10   (b) 12
(c) 15   (d) 18

Ans. (a) The Association of South-East Asian Nations or ASEAN, was established on 8th August, 1967 in Bangkok. Currently there are 10 members in the ASEAN.

(ii) What is the objective of the ASEAN?
(a) To increase competition among the members countries for better products.
(b) To integrate the economies of the region to make region more attractive for investors.
(c) To promote economic cooperation in South-East Asia and ensure economic stability in the region.
(d) Both (b) and (c)

Ans. (b) ASEAN nations want to promote economic cooperation in South-East Asia and ensure economic stability in the region and to integrate the economies of the region to make region more attractive for investors.

(iii) Grouping of countries committed to remove all barriers to the free flow of goods and services between themselves and also pursue independent external trade policies is called ....
(a) Economic Union   (b) Free Trade Area
(c) Special Trade Zone   (d) Common Trade Zone

Ans. (b) Free Trade Area

(iv) Which of the following is not an objective of ASEAN Economic Community?
(a) To create common market and production base within ASEAN states to aid social and economic development in the region.
(b) To improve the existing ASEAN Dispute Settlement Mechanism for resolving economic dispute.
(c) To create a Free Trade Agreement for investment, labour and services.
(d) To carry out the coordination of security and Foreign policy.

Ans. (d) To carry out the coordination of security and foreign policy.

(v) Which of the following country is not a member of ASEAN?
(a) Philippines   (b) Mauritius
(c) Thailand   (d) Singapore

Ans. (b) Mauritius is not a member of ASEAN. Members of ASEAN are Brunei, Cambodia, Indonesia, Laos, Malaysia, Myanmar, the Philippines, Singapore, Thailand and Vietnam.

PART 2
Subjective Questions

• Short Answer Type Questions

1. Mention any four common features of European Union. **[Delhi 2008, All India 2008]**

Ans. The features of EU are as follows

(i) EU's share of world trade is much larger than that of US allowing it to be more assertive in trade disputes with US and China.

(ii) It has evolved from economic union to political one. It has its own flag, anthem, founding date and currency.

(iii) Its economic power gives it influence over its closest neighbours and on Asia and Africa. It also functions as an important bloc in international economic organisation such as WTO.

(iv) EU has political, economic, diplomatic and military influence. GDP of EU is slightly larger than that of US.

2. The European Union has evolved over time from an economic union to more than nation state.

or Explain any four factors that make European Union an influential organisation.

or "European Union is a highly influential regional organisation". Justify the statement with any four suitable arguments. **[CBSE 2020]**

Ans. The European Union has evolved over time from an economic union to an increasingly political one and has started to act more as a nation state. Factors that make European Union an influential are given below

(i) The EU has economic, political, diplomatic and military influence all over the world.

(ii) The EU is the world's second biggest economy next to that of the US.

(iii) It also functions as an important bloc in international economic organisations such as the world trade organisation. Two members of the EU, Britain and France, hold permanent seats on the UN security council.

(iv) Militarily, the EU's combined armed forces are the second largest in the world.

(v) In many areas, its member states have their own foreign relations and defence policies.

(vi) EU has its own flag, anthem, founding date and common currency. The EU has tried to expand areas of cooperation while acquiring new members, especially from soviet block.

Thus, the given statement that European Union is a highly influential regional organisation is correct.

3. How did the Marshall Plan paved the way for the formation of OEEC (Organisation of European Economic Cooperation)?

Ans. In June 1947, the American Secretary of state George C Marshall announced the European Recovery Programme that offered financial assistance to 16 countries to Europe to rebuild their economics. It was done to revive the economics Europe with a view to open up prime markets.

The way for the formation of OEEC

Under the Marshall plan, the Organisation for European Economic Cooperation (OEEC) was established in 1948 to channel aid to the West European States. It became a forum where the Western European States began to cooperate on trade and economic issues. Though George C Marshall offered his plan to the East European Countries, their regions were incapable of taking any decision by themselves. The Soviet Union denouned the Marshall Plan as dollar imperialism and prevented the fund from flowing towards East Europe.

4. How can the Euro pose a danger to the US Dollar?

Ans. European Union has a great economic influence in the world market including the market of United States. Euro is the currency of EU, which pose a threat to the dominance of US Dollar because of the following reasons

• Share of EU in world trade is much larger than that of US and this is the reason why EU can be more assertive in trade disputes with US and China. Economic power of EU provides great influence over Asia, Africa and its close neighbours.

• Many countries have joined EU who are directly linked with US and carry Dollar as their currency. These countries can take economic programmes which are against interest of US.

• As the European Union functions as an important bloc in economic organisation, such as World Trade Organisation (WTO).

5. Name the pillars and the objectives of the ASEAN Community. **[NCERT]**

Ans. The three pillars of ASEAN Community are

• ASEAN Security Community
• ASEAN Economic Community
• ASEAN Socio-Cultural Community

Association of South-East Asian Nations (ASEAN) was created in 1967 with the following objectives

(i) **Primary Objective** It was to increase economic growth, which will result in social progress and cultural development of the ASEAN. Thus, this objective was related to economic, cultural and social perspectives.

(ii) **Secondary Objective** Under United Nation Charter, principles and rules of law have been stated. So, the secondary objective of ASEAN nations was to promote stability and regional peace based upon those rules and principles.

6. What do you mean by SAARC? Mention any of its objectives?

Ans. The South Asian Association of Regional Cooperation (SAARC) was created in 1985 as an expression of the region's collective decision to evolve a regional cooperative framework.

The objective of SAARC are as follows

(i) To promote the welfare of the people of South Asia and to improve their quality of life.

(ii) To promote and strengthen collective self reliance among the countries of South Asia.

(iii) To accelerate economic growth, social progress and cultural development in the region and to provide all individuals the opportunity to live in dignity and to realise their full potential.

(iv) To strengthen cooperation with other developing countries.

7. Write a short note on BRICS highlighting its formation and objectives.

Ans. BRIC was founded in 2006 in Russia. BRIC turned into BRICS after the inclusion of South Africa in its first meeting in the year 2009. The key objectives of BRICS are primarily to cooperate and distribute mutual economic benefits among its members besides non-interference in the internal policies of each nation and mutual equality. The twelfth conference of BRICS was concluded in Russia in 2020. It was chaired by Russian President Vladimir Putin.

The objectives of BRICS are summarised as follows

- The BRICS seeks to deepen, broaden and intensify cooperation within the grouping and among the individual countries for more sustainable, equitable and mutually beneficial development.

- BRICS takes into consideration for each member's growth, development and poverty objectives to ensure that relations are built on respective country's economic strength as well as to avoid competition where possible.

- To enhance and diversify trade and investment cooperation that support value addition among the BRICS countries.

- To enhance market access opportunities and facilitate market interlinkages.

8. What makes Russia a new centre of power or alternate centre of power?

Ans. The Russian Federation has been suggested as a potential candidate for resuming superpower status in the 21st century. Russia emerged as the strong successor of USSR. Some of the following aspects make Russia a new centre of power

- In terms of economic power, Russia is considered an 'energy superpower'. It has the world's largest proven natural gas reserves and is the largest exporter of natural gas and second largest producer of petroleum.

Russia has an abundance of oil, natural gas and precious metals, which make up a major share of Russia's exports.

- In terms of Military power, it is one of the world's largest military forces, making it the most powerful military in Europe. Russia was the sixth-largest nation in terms of military spends, at $61.4 billion.

- In terms of political and diplomatic powers, Russia is also a permanent member of the UN Security Council, called P-5. Russia is a part of many supranational organisations including the Group of Eight (G8), The Council of Europe, the Organisation for Security and Co-operation in Europe (OSCE), the Commonwealth of Independent States (CIS), and BRICS. Being the largest nation in terms of territory it automatically becomes a largest producer of some crucial resources and has a say on its neighbouring nations.

9. How Israel has emerged as a powerful nation in the 21st century? Discuss.

Ans. Israel has emerged as one of the most powerful nations in the 21st century in terms of science and technology, defence and intelligence. It has reached to the new heights of global political standing by virtue of its strong defence powers, technological innovations, industrialisation and agricultural development. It is a small Jewish- Zionist nation which is placed in the contemporary global politics in general and the Arab-dominated West Asian Politics in particular. In terms of economy, Israel is well- developed free market economy that is technologically advanced. After the United States, it has the world's second-largest number of startup enterprises. Its exports include diamonds, high-tech equipments and pharmaceuticals.

In terms of political and diplomatic power, Israel maintains full diplomatic relations and open borders with two of its Arab neighbours, Egypt and Jordan, after signing peace treaties in 1979 and 1994 respectively. Israel has been a member of the United Nations since 11th May, 1949. Israel also participates in other international organisations such as the International Atomic Energy Agency (IAEA) and the World Health Organisation (WHO).

10. How can we say that India is emerging as super-rational organisation? Examine.

Ans. The Republic of India is considered one of the emerging superpowers of the world. In 2015, India became the world's fastest growing economy with a 7.5% estimated GDP rate. The country must overcome many economic, social and political problems before it can be considered a superpower. Some of the following aspects can be considered that makes India a super-rational organisation

- In terms of economic power, it is the world's fifth-largest economy by nominal GDP and the third-largest by purchasing power parity. In 2019, India's ten largest trading partners were USA, China, UAE, Saudi Arabia, Hong Kong, Iraq, Singapore, Germany, South Korea and Switzerland. In 2018–19, the Foreign Direct Investment (FDI) in India was $64.4 billion.

- In terms of military power, Indian army is the third largest army in the world. It has also the fourth-largest defence budget in the world. India is also well equipped with nuclear arsenal.
- In terms of political and diplomatic power, India shares extremely positive relations through economic and political agreements with several Western, European, Asian and South-East Asian countries. India has also played an important and influential role in other international organisations like East Asia Summit. India is part of some very important emerging centres of power like BRICS, G20, SAARC etc.

11. What were the two major policy decisions taken by the Chinese leadership in the 1970s? **[All India 2016]**

or Describe any four new economic policies of China to make it grow at a faster rate. **[Delhi 2013]**

or Explain the new economic policies of China since 1978. **[All India 2013]**

Ans. China's economic success has been linked to its rise as a great power. The major policy decisions regarding new economic policies of China were

(i) China ended its political and economic isolation with the establishments of relations with the United States in 1972.

(ii) Four modernisations (agriculture, industry, science and technology and military) were proposed by the Premier Zhou Enlai in 1973.

(iii) Den Xiaoping declared the 'Open Door Policy' and rapid economic reforms in China. It was meant to generate higher productivity by investments of capital and technology from other countries.

(iv) The privatisation of agriculture in 1982 was followed by the privatisation of industry in 1998.

(v) The trade barriers were eliminated only in Special Economic Zones (SEZs) where foreign investors could set up enterprises.

12. In spite of improvement in the Chinese economy, there have been negative consequences affecting the people of China. Mention any four such consequences. **[Delhi 2016, All India 2016]**

or Highlight any four drawbacks in the changed Chinese economic system. **[Delhi (C) 2008]**

Ans. Even though the Chinese economy has improved dramatically, there have been negative consequences affecting the people of China. The four negative consequences or drawbacks in the changed Chinese economic system are

(i) The benefits of the reforms have not been equally received. Approximately 100 million people are still unemployed.

(ii) Female employment and conditions of work are as bad as in Europe of the 18th and 19th centuries.

(iii) Corruption and environmental degradation have increased.

(iv) There has been rise in economic inequality between rural and urban residents and coastal and inland provinces.

13. Analyse the basis of projection of China to overtake the US as the world's largest economy by 2040. **[Delhi 2009]**

Ans. China is viewed to dominate US by the year 2040. The basis of the projection are

- China is considered as the driver of East-Asian growth because of the economic integration into regions. China is considered to be very powerful and factors such as population, landmass, resources, regional location and political influence adds to its strength.
- China announced 'Open Door Policy' in 1978 which aimed at generation of high productivity by investments in capital and technology from abroad. In economic sector, various steps were taken to encourage investment by Western entrepreneurs for modernisation of industry, science and technology, agriculture and military. In 1980, China became the member of World Bank and International Monetary Fund.
- Privatisation of agriculture and industry helped in growing economy rapidly.
- Foreign trade grew with the creation of SEZs and new trading laws. This resulted in high foreign exchange reserves. In this way, China became most significant for FDI.
- The above points show China's ability to overtake US as world's largest economy by 2040.

14. How does geographical proximity influence the formation of regional organisations?

Ans. The geographical proximity influences the formation of regional organisations in the following ways

- It affects the parameters of security of all countries in particular regions by similar forces. Thus, the organisations are created mainly for security reasons.
- It promotes rise in same socio-cultural problems that leads to the formation of treaties between the countries like the formation of ASEAN.
- The economic issues also affects the merger of countries so that they can handle the economic problems of the respective regions by coalition of interests through an organisation like the European Union.

15. The emerging economies of China and India have great potential to challenge the unipolar world. Do you agree with the statement? Substantiate your arguments. **[NCERT]**

Ans. Yes, we agree with the statement that both India and China have great potential to challenge the unipolar world on the following grounds:

- The New Economic policies of India and China have broken their economies from stagnation.

- In China, the creation of Special Economic Zones led to a phenomenal rise in the Foreign Trade. On the other hand, India is being seen as an important emerging global power in the 21st century from a strategic perspective as it is self-sufficient with indigenous nuclear technology.
- Both the countries are important destination for Foreign Direct Investments.
- At the global level also both India and China has adopted similar policies in WTO to deepen their integration with the world economy as a challenge to a unipolar world.

• Long Answer Type Questions

1. What makes European Union a highly influential regional organisation?   **[NCERT]**

Ans. European Union is a highly influential organisation due to the following reasons

Economic Influence of EU

- EU is the world's second biggest economy with a GDP of more than $17 trillion in 2016, next to the United States of America.
- Its currency Euro can pose a threat to the dominance of US dollar. EU's share of world trade is much larger than that of US.
- It has an economic influence over its closest neighbours as well as in Asia and Africa.

Political and Diplomatic Influence of EU

- The EU also has political and diplomatic influence as two members of EU i.e. Britain and France, hold permanent seats in the UN Security Council with several non-permanent members.
- The EU is enabled to influence some US policies such as the current US position on Iran's Nuclear Programme.
- Its diplomacy, economic investment and negotiations have been effective as in the case of its dialogue with China on human rights and environmental degradation.

Military Influence of EU

- EU's combined armed forces are the second largest in the world and also come second after the total spending's of US in defence.
- Britain and France as EU members also possess nuclear arsenal of 550 nuclear warheads. It is also the world's second most important source of space and communication technology.
- EU is able to intervene in economic, political and social areas. But in many areas member states have their own foreign and defence policy that are often at odds with each other.

2. How did the European countries resolve their post-Second World War problem? Briefly outline the attempts that led to the formation of the European Union.   **[NCERT]**

Ans. After the Second World War, the European states confronted the ruin of their economies along with the destruction of assumptions and structure on which Europe had been founded. European countries resolved their Post Second World War problems in the following manner

- Under the Marshall Plan, the USA provided financial help to revive European economy.
- The US also created a new collective security structure under NATO.
- Under the Marshall Plan, the organisation for European Economic Cooperation was established in 1948 to extend cooperation on trade and economic issues among the Western European states.
- European Union was founded in 1993 for a common foreign security policy, cooperation on justice and home affairs and creation of a single currency.

The attempts led to the formation of European Union are as follows

- The Council of Europe was established in 1949 for political cooperation.
- The process of economic integration of European Capitalist countries led to the formation of European Economic Community in 1957.
- The collapse of Soviet Union put Europe on a fast track and resulted in the formation of European Union in 1992.

3. List the factors that limit the ability of the EU to act in matters of foreign relations and defence. What role has been played by European Union in solving the problems of the European countries?

Ans. European Union is a super national organisation but in many areas its member states have their own foreign relations and defence policies that are often at odds with each other. Factors that limit the ability of the EU to act in matters of foreign relations and defence are discussed below

- British Prime Minister Tony Blair supported the US led Iraq invasion and many new members made US led 'coalition of willing' whereas while Germany and France opposed American policy.
- There is also a 'Euro–Skepticism' in some parts of Europe about the EU's integrationist agenda. Thus for example, Britain's former Prime Minister, Margaret Thatcher kept the UK out of European Market.
- Denmark and Sweden have resisted in Maastricht Treaty and the adoption of Euro, the common European currency.

Role played by European Union in solving the problems of European Countries are discussed below

- The EU functions as an important bloc in international organisation as World Trade Organisation to intervene in economic areas.

- The EU has expanded areas of cooperation while acquiring new members especially from Soviet bloc.
- The EU has an influential role in the UN policies because its two members Britain and France hold permanent seats in the UN Security Council.
- The EU is influential in the areas of diplomacy, economic investments and negotiation.

4. What are the major difference between the SAARC and the European Union as alternative centres of power?   **All India 2011**

Ans. The difference between the SAARC and the European Union are as follows

SAARC	European Union
It was established with a view to evolve cooperation through multi-lateral means.	It was established by NATO to devise a plan in order to enable its 16 member nations in Europe to revive their economy which shattered in Second World War. It was observed as support to capitalism against communism/socialism.
There is no common institution to guide SAARC.	European Union is guided by common institutions such as European Commission, European Parliament, European Court to Justice, etc.
It shows reluctant attitude to sacrifice nation sovereignty.	It shows attitude of sacrificing national sovereignty for greater and united Europe.
SAARC nations prefer technology adoption rather than innovation. USA and China have undue interference in internal affairs of SAARC, as they provide technology to these nations.	European Union nations are driving for invention and innovation. This resists interference of technological advanced nations such as USA and China.
The nature of economy in SAARC is agriculture and manufacturing sector.	The nature of economy in European Union is knowledge based service sector.
A few member countries (e.g. Pakistan), due to their self-centred approach understand SAARC's efforts only favourable to India as it may invade their markets and influence their societies.	Its member countries have their own foreign relations and defence policies that are often adds with each other, e.g. Britain's Prime Minister was America's partner in Iraq invasion, whereas Germany and France opposed American policy.

5. What makes India an emerging power or a new centre of power? Discuss in detail.

Ans. India is considered one of the emerging superpowers of the world. In 2015, India became the world's fastest growing economy with a 7.5% estimated GDP rate. The country must overcome many economic, social and political problems before it can be considered a superpower. India has become the third largest economy in Asia to keep its high rate of growth.

Some of the essential aspects based on which India can be considered as the major emerging powers are discussed below

India as an Economic Power

- It is the world's fifth-largest economy by nominal GDP and the third-largest by purchasing power parity.
- In 2019, India's ten largest trading partners were USA, China, UAE, Saudi Arabia, Hong Kong, Iraq, Singapore, Germany, South Korea and Switzerland.
- India ranks second globally in food and agricultural production.
- The Indian IT industry is a major exporter of IT services with $180 billion in revenue and employs over four million people.
- It is the world's tenth-largest oil producer and the third-largest oil consumer. The Indian automobile industry is the world's fourth largest by production.

India as Military Power

- Indian army is the third largest army in the world.
- It has also the fourth-largest defence budget in the world.
- India is also well equipped with nuclear arsenal. It has recently purchased modern weapons and arms from USA.

India as Political and Diplomatic Power

- India shares extremely positive relations through economic and political agreements with several Western, European, Asian and South -East Asian countries.
- India has also played an important and influential role in other international organisations like East Asia Summit.
- India could almost become sixth permanent member of UNSC but the decision was vetoed by China.
- India is part of some very important emerging centres of power like BRICS, G20, SAARC etc.

6. Explain the factors responsible for the rise of the Chinese economy.   **[Delhi 2009]**

Ans. China is the third major alternative centre of power. It is the fastest growing economy. China at one time was based on Soviet model and at that time, it broke all the links with capitalist world. Following are the factors responsible for rise of Chinese economy

Use of Soviet Model China accepted the Soviet model and relied on its resources. China decided to substitute imports by domestic goods and create state owned heavy industries from capital produced by agriculture.

Development of Industrial Economy China used all its resources to develop an industrial economy. All citizens were provided education and health programmes.

Relationship With USA China established relation with USA in 1972. The integration of China's economy and the inter-dependencies that it has created has enabled China to have considerable influence with its trade partners like USA.

Modernisation Modernisation in field of agriculture, industry, military, science and technology were proposed. This policy helped the Chinese Economy to break stagnation.

Major Policies Announced Open Door Policy was announced by Deng Xiaoping in 1978, which aimed at generation of high productivity by investments in capital and technology from abroad.

Era of Privatisation Privatisation of agriculture in 1982 and privatisation of industry in 1998 was done. Privatisation led to remarkable rise in agricultural production and rural incomes. High personal saving in the rural economy lead to an exponential growth in rural industry. Both industry and agriculture grew at a faster rate.

Establishment of SEZ's Special Economic Zones were set up. State had a centralised role in setting up of China's economy. China become the most important destination for Foreign Direct Investment (FDI) any whwere in the world. It led to large forign reserves that now allow it to make big investment in other countries.

• Case Based Questions

1. Read the following passage carefully and answer the questions that follow.

ASEAN was and still remains principally an economic association. While the ASEAN region as a whole is a much smaller economy compared to theUS, the EU, and Japan, its economy is growing much faster than all these. This accounts for the growth in its influence both in the region and beyond. The objectives of the ASEAN Economic Community are to create a common market and

production base within ASEAN states and to aid social and economic development in the region. The Economic Community would also like to improve the existing ASEAN Dispute Settlement Mechanism to resolve economic disputes. ASEAN has focused on creating a Free Trade Area (FTA) for investment, labour and services. The US and China have already moved fast to negotiate FTAs with ASEAN.

(i) What is the objective of ASEAN Economic Community?

(ii) Why did ASEAN established Free Trade Agreements?

(iii) How would ASEAN Economic Community resolve economic dispute?

Ans. (i) The objective of ASEAN Economic Community is to create common market and production based activities within ASEAN state itself and to aid social and economic development.

(ii) ASEAN established FTA's for investment purposes and for labour services. FTA is an agreement between two or more countries where countries agree on certain obligations that affect trade in goods and services.

(iii) ASEAN Economic Community would resolve economic dispute by improving the existing ASEAN dispute settlement mechanism.

2. Read the following passage carefully and answer the questions that follow.

America extended massive financial help for reviving Europe's economy under what was called the 'Marshall Plan'. The US also created a new collective security structure under NATO. Under the Marshall Plan, the organisation for European Economic Cooperation (OEEC) was established in 1948 to channel aid to the West European States. It became a forum where the Western European States began to cooperate on trade and economic issues. The Council of Europe, established in 1949, was another step forward in political cooperation. The process of economic integration of European capitalist countries proceeded step by step leading to the formation of the European Economic Community (EEC) in 1957.

(i) What was Marshall Plan?

(ii) The US created a new collective security structure under which organisation?

(iii) Which organisation became a forum where the Western European states began to cooperate on trade and economic issues?

Ans. (i) A plan introduced by USA to provide financial help for the revival of European Economy. It was enacted in 1948 and provided more than $ 1.5 billion to help finance rebuilding efforts on the continent.

(ii) The US created a new collective security structure under NATO. NATO was created in 1949 that put the Western European nations under the nuclear umbrella of the US.

(iii) Organisation for European Military Cooperation became a forum where the Western European states began to cooperate on trade and economic issues.

3. Observe the picture given below and answer the following questions.

(i) In which year the bipolar structure of world politics ended? What became clear for America's dominance? Which two associations of nations emerged in Europe and Asia?

(ii) What is indicated by the first picture?

(iii) What is being indicated by the second picture?

Ans. (i) It was the year of 1990 in which bipolor structure of world politics ended.

It became clear that alternative centres of political and economic power could unite America's dominance.

Thus, in Europe, the European Union (EU) and in Asia, the Association of South-East Nations (ASEAN) have emerged as forces to reckon with.

(ii) The first picture here represents the beginning of the history of Red China (or Communist China). "The Socialist Road is the Broadest of All" represents the ideology that guided China during its early phase after the revolution took place in China in 1949. It tells that China's economy will become the largest economy of the world by 2040 because it prepared Soviet model of economy and always keeps capitalist ideas submissive to the same.

(iii) The second picture is that of the city of Shanghai. This new and beautiful city is the symbol of China's new economic power.

4. Study the picture given below carefully and answer the following questions.

(i) The given image refers to which policy of India since 1991?

(ii) Explain the significance of this policy as shown in the image above.

(iii) Evaluate India's role in ASEAN.

Ans. (i) The given image refers to the New Economic Policy of 1991.

(ii) The policy is related to economic liberalisation in India. This policy brought various changes to bring economic reforms such as expand in the private and foreign investment but it also resulted in reduction in import tariffs, deregulation of markets, etc.

This on one hand makes on economy market oriented but at the same time increase competition for domestic producers. But once the policy is adopted, India has to stay on the path and bear the costs of economic liberalisation and economic growth.

(iii) Association of South-East Asian Nation (ASEAN) was formed in 1967. India is a member of ASEAN, East Asia Summit has been pushing for the growth of trade relations. It is increasing its significance as a trading and investment partner to Thailand, Myanmar and Singapore.

India is looking forward to creating an area for free trade, investment, provision of labour and services.

India respects the national sovereignty of every country and believes in regional development. India has signed FTAs with two ASEAN members Singapore and Thailand.

Chapter Test

Objective Type Questions

1. For what purpose the Council of Europe has established?
    (a) Economic integration   (b) Security
    (c) Political cooperation   (d) Trade development

2. In the European flag circle of .... stars stands for ....
    (a) silver, harmony and peace   (b) bronze, solidarity and cooperation
    (c) gold, solidarity and harmony   (d) copper, peace and solidarity

3. Arrange the following in correct sequence.
    1. ASEAN Regional Forum   2. Unification of Germany
    3. Introduction of Euro Currency   4. European Union

    Codes
    (a) 1, 2, 4 and 3   (b) 2, 4, 1 and 3
    (c) 1, 4, 2 and 3   (d) 4, 3, 2 and 1

4. Consider the following statement(s) with regard to ASEAN community. Mark the correct option(s).
    (a) The ASEAN community has established three pillars.
    (b) It aims to uphold the regional or cultural sovereignty of the people.
    (c) It was established in 2004.
    (d) (a) and (b)

5. The headquarters of SAARC is located in ....
    (a) India   (b) Maldives
    (c) Nepal   (d) Bhutan

Short Answer Type Questions

1. What are the factors responsible for the rule of Chinese economy?

2. What do you know about 'Bangkok Declaration'?

3. How has been European Union able to influence the world?

4. State the components of ASEAN Vision 2020.

5. Mention some of the steps taken by China to improve its economy.

6. When was the ASEAN regional forum established? What were its main objectives?

7. What are the drawbacks in the changed Chinese economic system?

Long Answer Type Questions

1. Discuss the role of European Union as a supernational organisation.

2. Define ASEAN. What steps should be taken to strengthen it?

3. Elucidate the pillars of ASEAN. What are the objectives of ASEAN community?

4. Mention the significance of SAARC. What are limitations of SAARC as a forum for facilitating economic cooperation among South Asia countries.

5. How did the European countries resolve their post - Second World War problem? Briefly outline the attemps that led to the formation of the European Union.

Answers

1. *(a)*   **2.** *(c)*   **3.** *(b)*   **4.** *(d)*   **5.** *(c)*

CHAPTER 02

South Asia and The Contemporary World

In this Chapter...

- South Asia
- Democratisation in South Asia
- Conflicts and Efforts for Peace in South Asia

South Asia

South Asia is referred to as a group of seven countries namely **Bangladesh, Bhutan, India,** the **Maldives, Nepal, Pakistan** and **Sri Lanka** which stand for diversity in every sense and constitutes geo-political space. The Himalayas in North and the vast Indian Ocean, Arabian Sea and Bay of Bengal in South, West and East respectively provide a natural insularity (Separation) to the region.

This region is largely responsible for the linguistic, social and cultural distinctiveness of the sub-continent. Afghanistan and Myanmar are often considered as the part of this region. China is not considered as the part of this region but it plays an important role.

Various kinds of conflicts in this region are evident like border disputes, water-sharing disputes between the states of the region. Some other kinds of conflicts include insurgency, ethnic strife and resource sharing issues.

Various Political Systems in South Asia

Countries which are part of South Asia consist of different kinds of political systems. In terms of civil liberties available to the people of South Asian countries, the track record of most of these countries is highly disappointing.

A democratic system is established and maintained since independence in India and Sri Lanka. On the other hand, Pakistan and Bangladesh have experienced as both **civilian** and **military** rulers, in which Bangladesh maintained democracy since the Post-Cold War.

Since the Post-Cold War period, Pakistan began with democratic governments under **Benazir Bhutto** and **Nawaz Sharif**. Although it also suffered from a military coup in 1999 and later it was run by the civilian government since 2008.

Nepal was under the Constitutional Monarchy till 2006. Later in 2008, monarchy was abolished and democracy was established. Thus, we can say that democracy is becoming an accepted norm within South Asian region.

The two smallest country of the region i.e. Bhutan and Maldives are facing similar issues. Bhutan became a **constitutional monarchy** in 2008.

A multi-party democracy emerged under the leadership of the King. Maldives on the other hand was a Sultanate till 1968 when it was changed into a republic with a Presidential form of government. A multi-party system was introduced in 2005 after the Parliament voting. The **Maldivian Democratic Party** (MDP) dominates the political affairs of the island, MDP won the 2018 elections.

People in all these countries share the desire for democracy. Ordinary citizens in these countries support the institutions of representative democracy. Hence, democracy is preferred over other forms of government.

Democratisation in South Asia

The demand for democracy has gained momentum in the South Asian region in the recent years. Ordinary citizen, rich and poor, of various religions, embrace the concept of democracy and support representative democratic institutions. There is a widespread support for democracy in all these countries.

People view the idea of democracy positively and prefer democracy over any other form of government as they believed that democracy is suitable for the country.

The democratic experiences in each of these regions, except India is discussed below

Pakistan

With the framing of the Constitution of Pakistan, **General Ayub Khan** took over the administration and soon got himself elected. He renounced his office after the dissatisfaction from his rule and the military took over under **General Yahya Khan**. During Yahya Khan rule, Pakistan faced the Bangladesh crises and a war with India in 1971. Bangladesh (East Pakistan) emerged as an independent country.

After 1971, an elected government was formed under the leadership of Zulfikar Ali Bhutto, removed by General Zia-ill-Haq in 1977. Again in 1982, a pro-democracy protest was faced by Pakistan. A democratic government was established in 1988 under the leadership of **Benazir Bhutto**. She had to face competition between her party, Pakistan People's Party and the Muslim League.

Later on the history repeated and **General Pervez Musharraf** took the command in 1999 and removed **PM Nawaz Sharif**. General Pervez Musharraf got himself elected as the President in 2001. Since 2008, democratically elected leaders have been ruling Pakistan.

Factors Affecting Unstable Democracy in Pakistan

Several factors that led to Pakistan's failure in building a stable democracy were as follow

- Social dominance of **military**, **clergy** and **landowning aristocracy** were responsible for the frequent overthrow of elected government and establishment of military governments.

- The pro-military groups became more powerful over India-Pakistan's conflict. These groups are against the principles of political parties and democracy.

- There has been a strong sense of pro-democracy sentiment in the country.

- Absence of genuine international support for democratic rule has further encouraged the dominance of military. Like for instance, USA and other Western countries have encouraged the military's authoritarian rule for their own reasons.

The military administration in Pakistan has been considered as the protector of Western interests in West Asia and South Asia, given their concern of what they call **global Islamic terrorism** and the danger that Pakistan's nuclear program could fall into the hands of these terrorist groups.

Bangladesh

Bangladesh was a part of Pakistan from 1947 to 1971, which comprises of the partitioned areas of Bengal and Assam from British India. Western Pakistan domination such as in the form of imposition of Urdu was resented by the common people of Bangladesh. Protests were evident in the country since the partition against the unfair treatment towards the Bengali culture and language. A demand for fair representation and a fair share in political power was also demanded.

Emergence of Bangladesh

- **Sheikh Mujib-ur Rahman** was a leader who led the popular struggle against the domination of West Pakistan and demanded independence for Eastern region.

- During the 1970's elections, the **Awami League** under Sheikh Mujib-ur Rahman won all the seats in East Pakistan and secured a majority in the constituent assembly. But the government under West Pakistan leadership refused to call up the assembly. After this, Sheikh Mujib was arrested.

- Under the rule of Yahya Khan, thousands of people were killed to suppress the mass movements. Problems like large scale migration towards India emerged and it created a refugee problem for India.

- The people of East Pakistan were supported financially and militarily by the Indian Government for their independence. This led to a war between India and Pakistan in December 1971. The war ended with the surrender of Pakistan forces in East Pakistan and Bangladesh was formed as an independent nation.

Internal Conflicts in Bangladesh

The Constitution of Bangladesh was drafted with the faith in secularism, democracy and socialism. In 1975, the Constitution was amended to shift from the parliamentary to presidential form of government by Sheikh Mujib Ur Rahman. Through this he abolished all the political parties except his own Awami League, which further led to conflicts and tensions in the country.

Sheikh Mujib was assassinated in a military uprising in 1975 and Ziaur Rahman, formed his own **Bangladesh National Party**. He won the elections of 1979 and was also assassinated. Then, the military took over under Lt. General HM Ershad. The people of Bangladesh stood up for the demand of democracy. Some political activity on a limited scale was allowed by Ershad and in 1990 mass public protests led his government to step down. Since the elections in 1991, representative democracy has been working in Bangladesh.

Nepal

Nepal was a Hindu Kingdom and became constitutional monarchy in modern period. People of Nepal and the political parties wanted a more open and responsive system of government. The King of Nepal retained control over the government and restricted expansion of democracy with the help of army.

- In 1990, the king accepted the demand for new democratic constitution in response to pro-democratic movements.
- In 1990s, the maoist rebels led and armes aggression against the monarch and ruling regimes.
- In 2002, the king dismissed the elected government and implemented absolute monarchy.
- In 2006, there were massive countrywide pre-democracy protests which led to the first major victory when the king was forced to restore the House of Representatives that had been dissolved in April 2002.
- This was led by the Seven Party Alliance (SPA), the maoists and social activists.
- The maoist rebels have joined the interim government led by GP Koirala and in 2007 Nepal shifted to democracy.
- In 2008, elections were held in Nepal in which even the maoists took part.
- The maoist leader Pushpa Kamal Dahal or Prachanda became the new PM of Nepal in 2016. Sher Bahadur Deuba is the current Prime Minister and Bidhya Devi Bhandari is the President of Nepal.

Sri Lanka

Sri Lanka got its independence in 1948 and since then it has retained its democracy. The democratic set-up of Sri Lanka was disturbed by the ethnic conflict by the **Sinhalese** and **Tamil** people.

Sinhalese people were the largest ethnic group of Sri Lanka and after the independence this group dominated the politics of the state. Tamils were the people who had migrated from India to Sri Lanka and settled there. According to Sinhala nationalists, Sri Lanka should not give concessions to Tamils as this state belongs only to Sinhala's.

The neglect of Tamils concerns and interests resulted in militant Tamil nationalism. The militant organisation **Liberation Tigers of Tamil Eelam** (LTTE) was working since 1983 onwards with the army of Sri Lanka for a separate country belongs to Tamil people. The North-Eastern parts of Sri Lanka were controlled by LTTE.

Indian Government has from time-to-time tried to negotiate with the Sri Lankan Government to protect interests of Tamils in Sri Lanka. Further, in 1987 an accord was signed between both the countries to stabilise relations between Sri Lankan government and Tamils. Eventually, the Indian Army got involved into fight with LTTE. This incident was felt by the Sri Lankans as an attempt by India to interfere in the internal affairs of Sri Lanka.

In 1989, **Indian Peace Keeping Forces** (IPKF) was pulled out of Sri Lanka. Although, the Sri Lankan crises remained violent in nature. Scandinavian countries like Iceland and Norway tried to negotiate in these crises. Later, in 2009 the armed rebellion came to an end as LTTE was defeated.

Sri Lanka has gained considerable economic growth and recorded high levels of human development despite of the on-going conflict situations. Sri Lanka's achievement has been remarkable in the South Asian region. It is one of the first developing countries to successfully control the population growth and liberalise its economy. It has the highest Per Capita GDP for many years.

Maldives

Maldives, an island country attained full political independence from the British in 1965 and in 1968 a new republic was inaugurated and the Sultanate abolished. **Ibrahim Nasr** the country's first president was succeeded in 1978 by Maumoon Abdul Gayoom, who was re-elected to his sixth consecutive term in 2003. The Maldives became a member of the Commonwealth in 1982.

In the first years of the 21st century, Gayoom's government embarked on a long term plan to modernise and democratise the Maldives, particularly its economy and political system.

Begining in 2003, wide-ranging reforms were instituted to improve human rights and the system of governance. In 2008 a new constitution was adopted that established greater governmental checks and balances strengthened the powers of the legislature and judiciary and allowed women to run for presidency. In October 2008, former political prisoner Mohamed Nasheed was elected President, thus ending Gayoom's 30 years in office. The current President of Maldives is Ibrahim Mohamed Solin.

Conflicts and Efforts for Peace in South-Asia

Conflicts and tensions in South-Asian region have not diminished in the post Cold War era. Conflicts over internal democracy and ethnic disparities have already been mentioned. However, there are some important international conflicts. Due to India's strategic location in the region, It is involved in the majority of conflicts, which are discussed below

India and Pakistan

Both these countries represent very crucial conflicts of an international nature which are discussed below

- **Conflict over Kashmir** is the major issue between both the countries. Pakistan government always claimed Kashmir to be its part and same goes with Indian government. Wars took place over this issue between India and Pakistan in 1947-48 and 1965 failed to settle the dispute. The 1947-48 war led to the division of the province into Pakistan-occupied Kashmir and the Indian province of Jammu and Kashmir divided by the **Line of Control** (LoC). In 1971, India won decisive war against Pakistan but the Kashmir issue remained unsettled.

- Strategic issues conflicts are also evident among these countries like the control of the **Siachen Glacier** and over acquisition of arms. Both countries want to acquire more nuclear weapons and missiles against each other in the 1990's. For instance, in 1998 India conducted its nuclear explosion in **Pokharan**. Within few days Pakistan responded by carrying out nuclear tests in the **Chagai Hills**.

- Suspicious nature of both the governments led to border disruptions especially in the Kashmir region. Like Indian government blames the Pakistan government for nurturing violence and helping Kashmiri militants with arms, training, money and protection to carry out terrorist activities against India. The Indian Government also believes that Pakistan had aided the pro-Khalistani militants with arms and ammunitions during the period 1985-1995.

- Similarly Pakistan's spy agency ISI (Inter Services Intelligence) is considered to be involved in various anti-India campaigns in North-East India. Indian security agencies are blamed too with similar blames by the government of Pakistan.

- Both countries also have problems related to **sharing of Indus river waters**. With the help of World Bank in 1960, both countries negotiated over this issue.

- There are still some minor differences about the interpretation of the **Indus Waters Treaty** and the use of the river waters. The two countries are not in agreement over the demarcation line in Sir Creek in the Rann of Kutch.

Efforts Towards Peace and Cooperation

Still both the countries India and Pakistan are holding negotiations over many issues. Some of the efforts towards peace between both the countries are discussed below

- Confidence building measures has been signed between both the countries to minimise the tensions in terms of security.

- Social activities and prominent personalities collaborated to develop friendly atmosphere.

- Number of bus routes has been opened up between the countries.

- **Samjhauta Express**, was started in July 1976 to improve people-to-people connect between the two countries after the Shimla Agreement.

- Trade between two parts of Punjab have increased substantially and visas are provided more easily.

- Finalising of Kartarpur corridor has shown a ray of hope for starting of talks between India and Pakistan after the 2019 Pulwama terror attack.

India and Bangladesh

There are few differences prevailing between the Governments of India and Bangladesh over sharing the waters of Ganga and Brahmaputra.

Further, the Governments of India has differences with Bangladesh due to the following reasons

- Illegal immigration of Bangladeshi people.

- Bangladesh's support for anti-India Islamic fundamentalist groups.

- Bangladesh's refusal to allow Indian troops to move through its territory to North-Eastern India.

- Its decision not to export natural gas to India or allow Myanmar to do so through Bangladeshi territory.

Efforts Towards Peace and Cooperation

- Both the countries do cooperate on many issues despite their differences like the improving economic relation considerably.

- Bangladesh is a part of India's **Look East Policy** that wants to link up cooperating regularly South-East Asia through Myanmar.

- Both India and Bangladesh have cooperated regularly for issues like disaster management and environmental issues.

- In December 2020, India and Bangladesh signed seven agreements and also inaugurated three projects to deepen their partnership. It includes cooperation in the hydrocarbons sector, agriculture and textiles, high impact community development projects to be carried out by India, and trans-border elephant conservation.

India and Nepal

India and Nepal has developed a cordial and special relationship. The treaty between the countries allows the citizens of the two countries to travel and work in other country without visas and passports. Issues of conflict between India and Nepal are discussed below

- Indian government has often expressed displeasure at the warm relationship between Nepal and China.

- Indian security agencies have shown deep concerns over the Maoist movement in Nepal which however give rise to Naxalism in Bihar and Andhra Pradesh.

- The Nepal Government is in the notion that the Indian Government interferes in the internal affairs of Nepal and has designs on its river waters and hydro-electricity and prevents the landlocked country from getting access to the sea through Indian territory.

Efforts towards Peace and Cooperation

- Despite differences, trade, scientific, cooperation, common natural resources, electricity generation and interlocking water management grids hold the two countries together. India and Nepal relations are fairly stable and peaceful.
- South Asia's first cross-border petroleum products pipeline, constructed and funded by Indian Oil Corporation Ltd., connecting Motihari in India to Amlekhgunj in Nepal. It was inaugurated by the two Prime Ministers Narendra Modi and KP Sharma Oli on 10th September, 2019.

India and Sri Lanka

- The Government of India and Sri Lanka are mostly indulged in dispute over ethnic conflict in the island nation. The Indian leaders find it difficult to remain neutral when the Tamils are politically unhappy and are being killed.
- After the military intervention of 1987, the Indian Government has developed a policy of disengagement with Sri Lanka's internal troubles.

Efforts towards Peace and Cooperation

- There are steps and policies which have further strengthened ties between the two countries like the Free Trade Agreement and post-tsunami reconstruction in Sri Lanka.
- Sri Lanka is one of India's largest trading partners among the SAARC countries. India in turn is Sri Lanka's largest trade partner globally.
- Political relations between India and Sri Lanka have been marked by high-level exchanges of visits at regular intervals. In June 2019, the first overseas visit of Indian Prime Minister to Sri Lanka, in his second term, is an important symbolic gesture reflective of the special relationship between the countries.
- In April 2019, India and Sri Lanka also concluded agreement on countering Drug and Human Trafficking.

India and Bhutan

Some of the challenges faced by both India and Bhutan are discussed below

- For internal security perspective, illicit development of camps by militants in the dense-jungles of South-East Bhutan is a cause of concern for both the nations.
- Bhutan's concern regarding profitability of its Hydropower projects in the wake of India's shift to renewable sources of energy like wind, solar, etc.
- India and Bhutan enjoy a special relationship despite of major conflict. The effort of the Bhutanese Government to weed out the *guerrillas* and militants from North-East India has proved to be helpful to India.
- India is involved in big hydroelectric projects in Bhutan and remains its biggest source of development aid.

India and Maldives

India has a cordial relationship with the island nation of Maldives. India supported Maldives on its request, when some Tamil Sri Lankan soldiers attacked Maldives, the Indian Air Force and Navy quickly reacted against the invasion. India also contributed towards the island's economic development, tourism and fisheries.

Efforts Towards Peace and Cooperation

- A comprehensive Action Plan for Defence was also signed in April 2016 to consolidate defence partnership between India and Maldives.
- $800 million Line of Credit Agreement in March 2019 was signed between India and Maldives, for assisting Maldives to achieve sustainable social and economic development.

Conclusion

- India has various problems with its neighbours and given the size and power of India, they are bound to be suspicious of India's intention.
- The Indian Government often feels exploited and does not like the political instability in these countries which may provide platform for the outside powers to gain influence in the region. The smaller countries fear that India wants to be a regionally dominant power.

Chapter Practice

Objective Questions

• Multiple Choice Questions

1. .... and ...... established and maintained democratic system since independence.
(a) India, Pakistan
(b) India, Maldives
(c) India, Sri Lanka
(d) India, Nepal

Ans. (c) India and Sri Lanka established and maintained democratic system since independence.

2. ...... was under constitutional monarchy till 2006.
(a) Bhutan
(b) Maldives
(c) Bangladesh
(d) Nepal

Ans. (d) Nepal was under constitutional monarchy till 2006. Later in 2008, monarchy was abolished and democracy was established.

3. Which among the following was the first country to liberalise its economy in the South Asia region?
(a) Nepal
(b) Bhutan
(c) Sri Lanka
(d) Bangladesh

Ans. (c) Sri Lanka was the first country to liberalise its economy in the South Asian region. Sri Lanka got its independence in 1948 and since then it has retained democracy.

4. Which among the following statements about South Asia is wrong? **[NCERT]**
(a) All the countries in South Asia are democratic.
(b) Bangladesh and India have signed an agreement on river-water sharing.
(c) SAFTA was signed at the 12th SAARC Summit in Islamabad.
(d) The US and China play an influential role in South Asian politics.

Ans. (a) All countries in South Asia are not democratic and consists different kinds of political systems. South Asia stands for diversity in every sense and yet constitutes one geo political space.

5. Who took the administration after Pakistan framed its first constitution?
(a) General Zia-ul-Haq
(b) General Yahya Khan
(c) General Parwez Musharra
(d) General Ayub Khan

Ans. (d) General Ayub Khan took the administration after Pakistan framed its first constitution. He had to give up office when there was popular dissatisfaction against his rule.

6. Name the party which won 1970s election under Sheikh Mujib-ur-Rahman.
(a) Awami League
(b) Jaliya Party
(c) Bangladesh Nationalist Party
(d) Bangladesh People's League

Ans. (a) Awami League Party won 1970s election under Sheikh Mujib-ur-Rahman. He is also considered as the founding father of Bangladesh who led to struggle for its independence.

7. In which year the king of Nepal dismissed the elected government and implemented absolute monarchy?
(a) 2000
(b) 2003
(c) 2002
(d) 2004

Ans. (c) In 2002 the king of Nepal dismissed the government and abolished the Parliament.

8. Which two countries signed Indus Water Treaty with the World Bank as negotiator?
(a) India and Bangladesh
(b) India and Pakistan
(c) India and Afghanistan
(d) India and Nepal

Ans. (b) India and Pakistan signed Indus Water Treaty with World Bank as a negotiator. It was signed in 1960 by then PM Jawaharlal Nehru and President Ayub Khan.

9. Which among the following statements about the Ethnic conflict in Sri Lanka is incorrect?
(a) The neglect of Tamils concerns and interests resulted in militant Tamil Nationalism.
(b) Tamil people were the largest ethnic group of Sri Lanka.
(c) There was lack of political equality in Sri Lanka.
(d) Sinhalas were favoured as they dominated the politics of the state.

Ans. (b) Sinhalese people were the largest ethnic group of Sri Lanka and after the independence this group dominated the politics of the state.

10. Arrange the following in correct sequence.
 (i) Sri Lanka gains independence.
 (ii) Democracy restoration in Pakistan, Bangladesh and Nepal.
 (iii) Proclamation of Independence by leaders of Bangladesh.
 (iv) Pakistan joined the Cold War Military blocs SEATO and CENTO.

Codes
(a) (i), (iii), (iv) and (ii)   (b) (ii), (iii), (iv) and (i)
(c) (i), (iii), (ii) and (iv)   (d) (i), (iv), (iii) and (ii)

Ans. (d) The correct sequence is
 • Sri Lanka gains independence on 4th February, 1948.
 • Pakistan joined the Cold War Military blocs SEATO and CENTO in 1955.
 • Proclamation of independence by leaders of Bangladesh was on 25th March, 1971.
 • Democracy was restored in Pakistan, Bangladesh and Nepal in 2008.

11. Arrange the following in correct sequence.
 (i) South Asian Free Trade Agreement came into force.
 (ii) IPKF operation in Sri Lanka.
 (iii) India and Bangladesh signed Farakka Treaty.
 (iv) India's nuclear test in Pokhran.

Codes
(a) (i), (ii), (iii) and (iv)   (b) (iv), (ii), (iii) and (i)
(c) (iv), (i), (ii) and (iii)   (d) (iii), (ii), (iv) and (i)

Ans. (b) The correct sequence is
 • India's nuclear test in Pokhran—1974
 • IPKF operation in Sri Lanka—1987
 • India and Bangladesh signed Farakka treaty—1996
 • SAFTA came into force—2006

12. Consider the following statements are select the correct statement(s).
 (i) Sheikh Mujib was assassinated in 1975.
 (ii) Zulfikar Ali Bhutto was removed by General Zia-ul-Haq in 1976.
 (iii) Lt. general HM Ershad step down in Sri Lanka in 1990.
 (iv) General Parwez Musharraf removed PM Nawaz Shariff in 1999.

Codes
(a) Both (i) and (iv)   (b) Both (ii) and (iii)
(c) Both (i) and (ii)   (d) All of these

Ans. (a) Sheikh Mujib was assassinated in 1975.
 • Zulfikar Ali Bhutto was removed by General Zia-ul-Haq in 1977.
 • Lt Gen HM Ershad step down in Bangladesh in 1990.
 • General Parwez Musharraf removed Prime Minister Nawaz Shariff in 1999.

13. Consider the following statements are select the incorrect statement(s).
 (i) Bhutan became Constitutional Monarchy in 2008.
 (ii) Multiparty system was introduced in Maldives in 2004.
 (iii) India-Pakistan crises began in 1971.
 (iv) Zulfikar Ali Bhutto was removed in 1976.

Codes
(a) Both (i) and (iii)   (b) Both (ii) and (iv)
(c) Only (iii)   (d) Only (iv)

Ans. (b) Statement (ii) and (iv) are incorrect as Multiparty system was introduced in Maldives in 2005 and Zulfikar Ali Bhutto was removed in 1977.

14. Which among the following was earlier an island ruled by Sultan as the head of state and now it is a republic country?
(a) Sri Lanka   (b) Malaysia
(c) Maldives   (d) Indonesia

Ans. (c) Maldives was earlier an island ruled by Sultan as the head of state and now it is a republic country.

15. Which of the following country is related to the cartoon?
(a) Bangladesh   (b) Bhutan
(c) Nepal   (d) Pakistan

Ans. (d) The country related to the cartoon is Pakistan and it represents the dual role of Pakistan's Parvez Musharraf.

• Assertion-Reasoning MCQs

Directions (Q. Nos. 16-20) In the following questions, a statement of Assertion (A) is followed by a statement of Reason (R). Mark the correct choice as
(a) Both A and R are true and R is the correct explanation of A.
(b) Both A and R are true, but R is not the correct explanation of A.
(c) A is true, but R is false.
(d) A is false, but R is true.

16. Assertion (A) Despite the mixed record of the democratic experience, the people in all these countries share the aspiration for democracy.

Reason (R) A recent survey of the attitudes of the people in the five big countries of the region showed that there is widespread support for democracy in all these countries.

Ans. (a) Both A and R are true and R is the correct explanation of A as despite the mixed record of all democratic experience people wish to be ruled by representatives elected by them as a democratic government. As per the recent survey, People believe that democracy is suitable for their country as it is a legitimate government.

17. Assertion (A) Various countries in South Asia do not have the same kind of Political systems.

Reason (R) Despite many problems and limitations Sri Lanka and India have successfully operated a democratic system since their independence from the British.

Ans. (b) Both A and R are true, but R is not the correct explanation of A as various countries in South Asia do not have the same kind of political systems. In the case of India and Sri Lanka despite of frequent ups and downs they both managed their democratic status. The path to democracy for them was not easy but they overcome every obstacle to maintain stability in democracy.

18. Assertion (A) The Sri Lankan problem involves people of Indian origin and there is considerable pressure from the Tamil people in India to the effect that the Indian government should protect the interests of the Tamils in Sri Lanka.

Reason (R) The government of India has from time to time tried to negotiate with the Sri Lankan Government on the Tamil question.

Ans. (a) Both A and R are true and R is the correct explanation of A. The Indian intervention in the Sri Lankan Civil War was the deployment of the Indian Peace keeping force in Sri Lanka that intended to perform a peacekeeping role. India signed an accord with Sri Lanka and sent troops to stabilise relations between Sir Lankan Government and the Tamils.

19. Assertion (A) Bhutan never became a constitutional monarchy.

Reason (R) Under the leadership of the king, Bhutan emerged as a multi-party democracy.

Ans. (d) A is false as Bhutan became a constitutional monarchy is 2008. R is true as this happened under the leadership of king and Bhutan emerged as a multi-party democracy.

20. Assertion (A) Democratic government had a short and troubled career.

Reason (R) India continued to enjoy domocratic status since its inception. It is considered to be among the best domocracies of the world.

Ans. (b) A is false, but R is true as it depends upon the leaders of the nation whether the country enjoys the democratic status for longer period of time or not. In the case of Indian politics, it had never tried to curb the Fundamental Rights of the people. Due to this fact, India is considered to be among the best democracies of the world.

• Case Based MCQs

1. Study the following and answer the questions.

Nepal's transition to democracy is almost complete. Nepal has undergone a unique moment in its history because it formed a Constituent Assembly to Let's know more draft the constitution for Nepal. Some sections in Nepal thought that a nominal monarchy was necessary for Nepal to retain its link with the past. The Maoist groups agreed to suspend armed struggle.

They wanted the constitution to include the radical programmes of social and economic restructuring. All the parties in the SPA did not agree with this programme. The Maoists and some other political groups were also deeply suspicious of the Indian Government and its role in the future of Nepal. In 2008, Nepal became a democratic republic after abolishing the monarchy. In 2015, it adopted a new constitution.

(i) Why it is said that Nepal is undergoing a unique movement in its history?
  (a) As it is moving towards the formation of Constituent Assembly that will write the constitution.
  (b) As it is moving towards uncivilised protests and movement.
  (c) Due to nominal monarchy in Nepal.
  (d) None of the above

Ans. (a) Nepal is undergoing a unique movement in its history as it is moving towards the formation of Constituent Assembly that will write the constitution.

(ii) What is the desire of Maoist groups in Nepal?
  (a) The have agreed to suspend armed struggle.
  (b) They want the constitution to include the radical programmes of social and economic restructuring.
  (c) They were deeply suspicious on the intentions of Indian Government.
  (d) Both (a) and (b)

Ans. (b) The desire of Maoist groups in Nepal is that they want the constitution to include the radical programmes of social and economic restructuring.

(iii) Why were some political parties suspicious in Nepal?
  (a) Political groups were deeply suspicious regarding the role of Indian government in the future of Nepal.
  (b) Because they were against the democratic set-up.
  (c) Because they were suspicious regarding the social restructuring.
  (d) All of the above

Ans. (d) Some political parties were suspicious in Nepal as they were not sure of role on Indian Government in future of Nepal, they were against democratic set up and social restructuring.

(iv) In the above passage, SPA stands for ......
  (a) State Party Alliance   (b) Seven Party Alliance
  (c) Static Party Alliance   (d) Six Party Alliance

Ans. (b) In the above passage, SPA stands for Seven Party Alliance. Seven Party Alliance was a coalition of seven Nepali Political Parties who wanted to end the autocratic rule in the country.

(v) Why Nepal is important for India?
  (a) Because Nepal is a buffer state between India and China.
  (b) Because of internal security as Nepal shares a long open border with India.
  (c) Due to socio-economic development.
  (d) All of the above

Ans. (b) Nepal is important for India due to the following reasons

- Nepal has a strategic importance as it is a buffer state between India and China.
- Nepal shares a long open border with India and this can become a threat to India's internal security.
- Nepal helps in socio-economic development of bordering states especially Bihar and Uttar Pradesh.

PART 2
Subjective Questions

• Short Answer Type Questions

1. Despite the mixed record of democratic experience, the people of all the countries of South Asia share the aspiration of democracy.   **[Delhi 2012]**

or 'Democracy is becoming the first choice of the people of South Asia'. Justify the statement.

[All India 2015]

or Despite the mixed record of democratic experience, why do the people in South Asian countries, even today, share the aspiration in favour of democracy? Explain with the help of examples.

Ans. The various countries in South Asia have experienced mixed record of democracies. The people also shared aspirations for democracy to be flourished not only in rich or developed countries but in developing and underdeveloped countries also which can be drawn from the examples of Nepal, Pakistan, Bangladesh, Bhutan and Maldives because

- Every ordinary citizen, rich or poor belonging to different religions view the idea of democracy positively and support the institution of representative democracy.
- They prefer democracy over any other form of democracy and think that democracy is suitable for their country.

2. How are the external powers influencing bilateral relations in South Asia? Take any one example to illustrate your point.

Ans. The external powers are influencing bilateral relations in South Asia like. China and United States remain a key player in South Asian politics. America has been influencing the bilateral relations in South Asia since the end of the Cold War in the following ways

- The United States has worked as a moderator in Indo-Pakistan relations.
- Economic reforms and liberal economic politics in both the countries have increased the American participation.
- The South Asian diaspora are working in USA and this gives America added stake in the future of regional security and peace.

3. Analyse the common problems of South Asian countries.   **[All India 2011]**

Ans. South Asia includes countries like India, Pakistan, Bhutan, Bangladesh, Nepal, Maldives and Sri Lanka. The various natural areas such as Himalayas, Arabian Sea, Bay of Bengal, Indian Ocean are part to this region.

The common problems among them are

- **Poverty** All countries of South Asia suffered from large masses living in poverty. In India, nearly 22 percent people are living under poverty as per 2011-12 census.
- **Violation of Human Rights** There exists a great threat to human rights from anti-social elements, communalists and from people with negative attitude, thinking and approach.
- **Problem Faced by Democracy** Several countries of South Asia aspire to be a democratic country, but face a problem of stable democracy.
- **Women Empowerment** Women are generally seen at lower position in most of the South Asian nations. They are restricted and are not as free as their counterparts.

4. Describe the crucial conflicts between India and Pakistan.

Ans India and Pakistan represent very crucial conflicts of an international nature that are discussed below

(i) **Kashmir Dispute** After the partition, the two countries got embroiled over the fate of Kashmir. Wars between India and Pakistan in 1947-48 and 1965 failed to settle the matter. The 1947-48 war resulted in division of the province into Pakistan Occupied Kashmir (POK) and the Indian Provinces of Jammu and Kashmir divided by LOC.

(ii) **Bangladesh Issue** In 1971, there was a war between India and Pakistan over the question of liberation of Bangladesh (Former East Pakistan). In 1971 the war continued for about two weeks and then Pakistans Army General surrendered unconditionally to India and the Bangladesh Liberation forces.

(iii) **Arms Race** Arms race between the two countries assumed a new character with both states acquiring nuclear weapons and missiles to deliver such arms against each other in the 1990s. In 1998, India conducted nuclear explosion in Pokhran and Pakistan responded by carrying nuclear test in Chagai Hills.

5. Mention some of the recent agreements between India and Pakistan. Can we be sure that the two countries are well on their way to a friendly relationship?   **[NCERT]**

Ans. The agreements between India and Pakistan are as follows

- The two countries have agreed to undertake confidence building measures to reduce the risk of war.
- A number of bus routes have been opened up between the two countries.
- A train service has started operating between two countries.

- Finalising of Kartarpur Corridor has shown a ray of hope for initiation of talks between India and Pakistan after the 2019 Pulwama Terror Attack.

No doubt, efforts are being made to have a durable peace but there is little possibility of friendly relationship because Kashmir continues to be the main problem between the two countries. Pakistan is also responsible for terrorist activities in India such as Bombay blasts. Such actions on the parts of Pakistan are obstacles in the way of friendly relations between the two countries.

Therefore, the two countries are not well on their way to a friendly relationship.

6. What are some of the commonalities and differences between Bangladesh and Pakistan in their democratic experiences? **[NCERT]**

Ans. Commonalities between Bangladesh and Pakistan are

- There is majority of Muslim population in both countries.
- There have been military take over in both countries from time to time.
- There have been pro-democracy movements in both the countries.

Differences between Bangladesh and Pakistan are

- The US and Western countries have encouraged military's despotic rule in Pakistan in the past for their own interest. It is not so in case of Bangladesh.
- Pakistan is a nuclear power state but Bangladesh is not.
- In Pakistan, military, clergy and land-owning aristocrats dominated socially to overthrow elected governments whereas in Bangladesh, the leaders and their party members dominated for the same.

7. Discuss the issues of disagreements and disputes between India and Bangladesh.

Ans. The era of cordial relations between India and Bangladesh weakened after Sheikh Mujibur Rahman's assassination in 1975. There have been disagreements and disputes between the two countries on number of issues. Some of the issues are discussed below:

- Indian Government has differences with Bangladesh's denial of illegal immigration to India. This problem is not related only to land and employment in the states of Assam, Tripura and West Bengal rather it poses a threat to India's security as well.
- Bangladesh's support for anti-Indian Islamic fundamentalist groups is discouraging as it indirectly promotes violence.
- Bangladesh's refusal to allow Indian troops to move through its territory to North-Eastern India.
- Its decision not to export natural gas to India or allow Myanmar to do so through Bangladeshi territory.
- Bangladesh is increasingly being used for drug trafficking which dispatches opium from Burma and other countries of the Golden Triangle, to different destinations.

8. Mention two areas each of cooperation and disagreement between India and Bangladesh. **[NCERT]**

or Explain any two points of cooperation as well as confrontation each between India and Bangladesh.

Ans. Two areas of cooperation are as follows

(i) Bangladesh is a part of India's 'Look East Policy' that wants to link up with South-East Asia through Myanmar.

(ii) On disaster management and environmental issues, the two states have cooperated regularly.

Two areas of disagreement are as follows

(i) Dispute over sharing of the Ganga and Brahmaputra river waters.

(ii) The Indian Government has been unhappy with Bangladesh's denial of illegal immigration to India.

9. Describe the series of events that led to the formation of Bangladesh.

Ans. The series of events that led to the formation of Bangladesh are discussed below

- The people of East Pakistan (now Bangladesh) resented the domination of West Pakistan in the form of imposition of Urdu language.
- Protests were evident in the country since the partition against the unfair treatment towards the Bengali culture and language. They also demanded a fair representation in administration and a fair share in political power.
- Sheikh Mujib-ur Rahman led the popular struggle against West Pakistani domination. He demanded automomy from the Eastern region. In 1970 elections, Awami League under Sheikh Mujibur Rahman won all the seats in East Pakistan and secured a majority in the Constituent Assembly
- Government under Yahya Khan in West Pakistan refused to call up the Assembly and after this Sheikh Mujib - ur Rahman was arrested.
- Mass movements were suppressed by the West Pakistan which led to large scale migration towards India.
- The Government of India supported the demands of East Pakistan which resulted in a war between India and Pakistan in December 1971. It ended in the formation of Bangladesh.

10. "Nepal and India enjoy a very special relationship that has very few parallels in the world". Justify the statement with any three suitable arguments.

Ans. Nepal and India share a very special relationship that can be illustrated with three suitable examples as follows

(i) A treaty between the two countries allows the citizens of the two countries to travel and work in each other countries without visas and passports.

(ii) Nepal being a landlocked country enjoys easier access to sea through Indian territory for the purpose of trade and commerce with other nations.

(iii) Both countries share together trade, scientific cooperation, common natural resources, electricity generation and interlocking water management grids.

11. Name the principal players in the ethnic conflict in Sri Lanka. How do you assess the prospects of the resolution of this conflict?　　**[NCERT]**

Ans. The principal players in the ethnic conflict in Sri Lanka are the Sinhala community and Tamils who had migrated from India to Sri Lanka and settled there. The Sinhala nationalists are in majority and they do not want to give any concessions to Tamils who are in minority. This has led to militant Tamil nationalism and the LTTE has been fighting an armed struggle with Sri Lankan army since 1983. Their demand is of Tamil Eelam of a separate country for the Tamils of Sri Lanka.

However, the following crisis should be resolved with utmost diplomacy as possible. The government of Sri Lanka should provide the fundamental and basic rights to the Tamil population constitutionally and uphold the principle of democracy. It should also provides special status to the Tamil province for their rejuvenation and maintain peace and tranquility in the province and the country.

12. Countries of South Asia do not trust each other in various aspects. This region is unable to exert its influence at International level. Justify the statement and suggest measures to strengthen South Asia.

Ans. The given statements is true as the countries of South Asia do not trust each other especially in case of India they are highly supicious. Following are the two examples to justify the statement.

(i) India-Pakistan are powerful countries of South Asia. Both countries are involved in various conflicts and differences after partition and hence, they do not trust each other. Suspicious nature of both countries led to border disruptions especially in the Kashmir region. Indian government blames the Pakistan government for nurturing violence and helping Kashmiri militants with arms, training, money and protection to carry out terrorist activities aginst India.

(ii) There are tensions between India and Sri Lanka. The settlement of Indian Tamils in Sri Lanka is the main reason behind the tensions. Indian peace keeping force was sent to resolve matter but was pulled out as it was criticised by Sri Lankans. This issue has not been resolved yet.

Following are the ways to strengthen South Asia

- To unite countries of South Asia by resolving all differences.
- To take initiative to make South Asia economically strong.
- To use powers of nuclear countries like India and Pakistan for peaceful purposes.
- To peacefully resolve mutual problems instead of using armed forces.

13. Mention two areas of cooperation and disagreement between India and Nepal.

Ans. Two areas of cooperation are discussed as follows

- Both countries work in cooperation in areas of trade, scientific, common natural resources, electricity generation and interlocking water management grids. India and Nepal relations are fairly stable and peaceful.
- South Asia's first cross-border petroleum products pipeline, constructed and funded by Indian Oil Corporation Ltd. Connecting Motihari in India to Amlekhganj in Nepal was remotely inaugurated by Prime Minister Narendra Modi and KP Sharma Oli on September, 2019.

Two areas of disagreements are discussed as follows

- The Nepal Government is in the notion that the Indian Government interferes in the internal affairs of Nepal had designs on its river waters and hydro-electricity and prevents the landlocked country from getting access to the sea through Indian Territory.
- Indian security agencies have shown deep concerns over the maoist movement in Nepal which however give rise to naxalism in Bihar and Andhra Pradesh.

14. Discuss the relations of India and Sri Lanka in detail.

Ans. The relations between India and Sri Lanka are discussed below

- In recent years, the relationship has been marked by close contacts at all levels. Trade and investment have grown and there is cooperation in the fields of infrastructure development, education, culture and defence.
- There are steps and policies which have further strengthened ties between the two countries like the Free Trade Agreement and Post-Tsunami reconstruction in Sri Lanka.
- Political relations between India and Sri Lanka have been marked by high-level exchanges of visits at regular intervals. In June 2019, the first overseas visit of Indian Prime Minister to Sri Lanka, in his second term, is an important symbolic gesture that reflects special relationship between the countries.
- In April 2019, India and Sri Lanka also concluded agreement on countering Drugs and Human Trafficking.
- In recent years, significant progress in implementation of developmental assistance projects has further enhanced the bonds of friendship between the two countries.

15. Discuss the relations of India and Maldives and its importance for India.

Ans. India has a cordial relationship with the island nation of Maldives. Bilateral relations have been nurtured and strengthened by regular contacts at all levels. Through the decades, India has rushed emergency assistance to the Maldives, whenever sought.

- India has supported Maldives on its request, when some Sri Lankan soldiers attacked Maldives, the Indian Air force and Navy quickly reacted against the invasion.
- The 2004 tsunami and the drinking water crisis in male a decade later were other occasions when India rushed assistance.
- Given the geographical limitations imposed on the Maldives, India has exempted the nation from export curbs on essential commodities.

Maldives holds strategic importance for India due to its location in the Indian Ocean. While the Indian Ocean is considered as the key highway for global trade and energy flow, Maldives virtually stands as a toll gate. A favourable and positive maritime environment in the Indian Ocean is essential for the fulfillment of India's Strategic priority. Thus, India continuously aims at promoting an ever-expanding area of peace and stability around it. In addition, Maldives is an important partner in India's role as the net security provider in the Indian Ocean Region.

• Long Answer Type Questions

1. Analyse the working of democracy in Pakistan.

Ans. With the framing of the first Constitution of Pakistan, General Ayub Khan took over the administration and soon got himself elected. He renounced his office after the dissatisfaction from his rule and the military took over under General Yahya Khan. During Yahya Khan's military rule, Pakistan faced Bangladesh crisis and war with India in 1971 and East Pakistan was liberated as an independent country named Bangladesh.

After this, an elected government was formed under the leadership of Zulfikar Ali Bhutto from 1971 to 1977. The government of Zulfikar Ali Bhutto was removed by General Zia-ul-Haq in 1977 who had to face pro-democracy movement from 1982 onwards. Again in 1988, an elected democratic government was established under Benazir Bhutto but had to face competition between her party, Pakistan People's Party and the Muslim League.

However, the duration of elective democracy was short lived and again the military intervened in 1999 and General Parvez Musharraf removed the then Prime Minister, Nawaz Sharif in 2001 and got himself elected as the President.

2. Like India, why could democracy not take roots in Pakistan despite the fact that both the countries share a common past? **[All India 2011]**

or Explain the factors responsible for Pakistan's failure in building a stable democracy. Describe any two pro-democracy factors present in Pakistan which can pave the way for establishing a lasting democratic set-up over there. **[All India 2010]**

Ans. Pakistan does not have a good experience with democracy. Several factors contributed to failure in building a stable democracy in Pakistan. They are as follows

- There was always social dominance of military, clergy and landowning aristocracy which resulted in downfall of democratic government and existence of military government.
- Due to Pakistan's conflict with India, pro- military groups in Pakistan got strengthened. According to these pro-military groups, political parties and democracy is defective and there is a chance of harm to the security of Pakistan by narrow minded parties and disorganised democracy. And this way, justification for army's stay in power is provided.
- Lack of international support has been there in Pakistan for democratic rule.
- US and some Western countries moved Pakistan towards authoritarian rule for their own benefits. Military rule in Pakistan is supposed to be the protector of Western interests in West Asia, South Asia as 'Global Islamic Terrorism' and nuclear arsenal can only be controlled by military.

Even though, democracy has not been fully successful in Pakistan, there has been a strong pro-democracy sentiment in the country. Pakistan has a courageous and relatively free press and a strong human rights movement.

3. How is democratisation going on in Nepal since 1990? **[All India 2013]**

Ans. The pro-democracy movements forced the king to allow new democratic constitution in 1990. But it had a short and troubled career. There was a huge influence of Maoists in many parts of Nepal who believed in armed insurrection against the monarch and the ruling elite.

Hence, a triangular conflict among the Monarchist forces, the democrats and the Maoist took place for sometime.

The Parliament was abolished and the government was dismissed by the king in 2002. Again in 2006, the king was forced to restore the House of representatives after a massive country wide pro-democracy protests.

The Constituent Assembly was formed to write the constitution for Nepal. The constitution has come into effect with some amendment process going on.

In 2008 Nepal become a democratic republic after abolishing monarchy In 2015 it adopted a new constitution.

4. Explain the ethnic conflict in Sri Lanka and any two consequences of it. **[CBSE 2019]**

Ans. The democratic setup of Sri Lanka was disturbed by the ethnic conflict among the Sinhalese and Tamil origin people.

The bone of contention was the region of Ceylon which was represented by the majority Sinhala group. They opposed the migration and settlements of Tamilians from India in their region. According to the group, Sri Lanka was only for Sinhala people and not for Tamils.

This attitude of Sinhala people led to the establishment of Liberation Tigers of Tamil Eelam (LTTE), a militant organisation, which desired for a separate country.

The consequences of ethic conflict led to the following situations

- There was a pressure on the Government of India by the Tamils of Indian origin to intervene in the matter. Hence, the Government of India tried to negotiate with the Government of Sri Lanka on Tamil's question. But direct involvement was in the year 1987. India conceded to sent troops to Sri Lanka for the preservation of relations between Tamils and Sri Lanka Government. Eventually, the Indian troops got into a fight with LTTE.
- The presence of Indian troops was not liked by many Sri Lankans and hence in 1989, the Indian Peace Keeping Force (IPKF) pulled out of Sri Lanka without attaining its objective.

5. India's neighbours after think that the Indian Government tries to dominate and interfere in the domestic affairs of smaller countries of the region. Is this a correct impression? Discuss the factors responsible for it and how this perception can be curbed?   **[NCERT, All India 2011]**

Ans. No, this is not a correct impression. India never wanted to dominate or interfere in the domestic affairs of the smaller countries of the region. India believed that there are real economic benefits for all, if all the countries lift up trade barriers.

Various factors are responsible for the thinking of smaller countries of South Asia towards India which are as follows

- Due to size of India smaller countries are bound to be suspicious about India's intentions.
- Interference of India in internal affairs of Pakistan and helping in transformation of East Pakistan to Bangladesh into an independent country is another reason.
- These countries think that India wants to invade and dominate international markets with the help of SAFTA.

The thinking/perception of smaller countries could be cleared by the following facts

(i) India has always provided shelter to refugees those who came from different countries.

(ii) India has always cooperated with their neighbours like it has provided assistance to Bangladesh during floods, it has provided military help to Maldives during military attrack on the Maldives.

(iii) India has given an open invitation to SAARC countries to sell their products whout any trade tariffs.

• Case Based Questions

1. Read the following passing carefully and answer the questions that follow.

General Ayub Khan took over the administration of the country and soon got himself elected. He had to give up office when there was popular dissatisfaction against his rule. This gave way to a military takeover once again under General Yahya Khan. During Yahya's military rule, Pakistan faced the Bangladesh crisis and after a war with India in 1971, East Pakistan broke away to emerge as an independent country called Bangladesh.

After this, an elected government under the leadership of Zulfikar Ali Bhutto came to power in Pakistan from 1971 to 1977. The Bhutto government was removed by General Zia-ul-Haq in 1977. General Zia faced a pro-democracy movement from 1982 onwards and an elected democratic government was established once again in 1988 under the leadership, of Benazir Bhutto. In the period that followed, Pakistani politics centred around the competition between her party, the Pakistan People' Party and the Muslim League.

This phase of elective democracy lasted till 1999 when the army stepped in again Minister Nawaz Shariff. In 2001, General Musharraf got himself elected as the President. Pakistan continued to be ruled by the army, through the army rulers have held some elections to give their rule a democratic image. Since 2008, democratically elected leaders have ruling Pakistan.

(i) Pakistan's first constitution was enacted by the Constituent Assembly in which year?

(ii) Who removed Zulfikar Ali Bhutto and When?

(iii) Why democracy isn't stable in Pakistan?

Ans. (i) Pakistan's first constitution was enacted by the Constituent Assembly in 1956.

(ii) Zulfikar Ali Bhutto government was removed by General Zia - Ul - Haq in 1977.

(iii) Since its independence, Pakistan's system has fluctuated between civilian and military governments at various times throughout its political history, mainly due to political instability, civil-military conflicts and political curruption by the military establishment.

2. Read the following passing carefully and answer the questions that follow.

The Sri Lankan problem involves people of Indian origin and there is considerable pressure from the Tamil people in India to the effect that the Indian government should protet the interests of the Tamil in Sri Lanka. The government of India has from time to time tried to negotiate with the Sri Lankan government on the Tamil question.

But in 1987, the government of India for the first time got directly involved in the Sri Lanka Tamil question. India signed an accord with Sri Lank and sent troops to stablise relations between the Sri Lankan government and the Tamils. Eventually, the Indian Army got into a fight with the LTTE. The presence of Indian troops was also not liked much by the Sri Lankans.

They saw this as an attempt by India to intere in the internal affairs of Sri Lanka. In 1989, the Indian Peace Keeping Force (IPKF) pulled outof Sri Lank without attaining its objective. The Sri Lankan crisis continued to be violent. However, international actors, particulary the Scandinavian countries such as Norway and Iceland tried to bring the warring groups back to negotiations. Finally, the armed conflict came to end, as the LTTE was vanquished in 2009.

(i) Why was there a pressure of Indian Tamils to protect and safeguard the interests of Tamil living in Sri Lanka?

(ii) When did Government of India directly got involve in the conflict of Sri Lanka?

(iii) Who posed challenge to Indian Army in Sri Lanka?

Ans. (i) There was a pressure of Indian Tamils to protect and Safeguard the interest of Tamil living in Sir Lanka because the conflict in Sri Lanka involved people of Indian origin.

(ii) In 1987 the government of India directly got involved in the conflict of Sri Lanka.

(iii) The LTTE posed challenge to the Indian Army in Sir Lanka. LTTE stands Liberation Tigers of Tamil Eelam.

3. Observe the cartoon given below and answer the questions that follow.

(i) Interpret the role of two key players who are also interested in the region.

(ii) Is there any commonality between their perspective?

(iii) What does the second cartoon represent?

Ans. (i) China and USA are the two key players in the region. Sino-Indian relations have improved significantly during the last ten years. As shown in the cartoon, two leaders from India and China are exchanging agreements regarding trade, commerce and economy. It is being resented by Pakistan who wants China to stick to 'Core' issues (border issue) with India.

(ii) Both China and USA wants to have economic ties i.e. trade and commerce in the region in this age of liberalisation and globalisation.

(iii) Second cartoon represents the role of USA in South Asian region. The US has good relations with both India and Pakistan and therefore work as a moderator in India-Pakistan relations. In the cartoon, the US has been shown as a reference in tennis match between India and Pakistan.

4. Study the picture and answer the following questions

(i) What does the cartoon represent?

(ii) "I'm always good at calculations". What does this represent?

(iii) How is the system of governance in India different from that of the country related to the cartoon?

Ans. (i) These equations speak about dominance of one person militarily more rather than only President.

(ii) It shows to the nation that Musharraf wants to command the country militarily and administratively both to strenthen his power because President's survival is not easy without military power.

(iii) The difference between India and Pakistan does not appear to be in the system of government as both have constitutions that enshrine federal republic system of government. The difference between the two appears to be a culture of democracy that has evolved in India over the last 57 years, while in Pakistan democracy remains still born.

Chapter Test

Objective Type Questions

1. Which two countries have a democratic system since their independence from British?
    (a) Bhutan and Pakistan   (b) Sri Lanka and Nepal
    (c) India and Sri Lanka   (d) Pakistan and Bangladesh

2. In which year Nepal became the democratic republic?
    (a) 2006   (b) 2007   (c) 2008   (d) 2009

3. It is one of the first developing countries to successfully control the population growth. It is ....
    (a) Nepal   (b) Bhutan   (c) Sri Lanka   (d) Pakistan

4. How many agreements are signed between India and Bangladesh in December 2020?
    (a) Five   (b) Seven   (c) Eight   (d) Nine

5. LTTE stands for ....
    (a) Legal Tigers of Tamil Entity   (b) Legal Tigers of Tamil Eelam
    (c) Liberation Tigers of Tamil Election   (d) Liberation Tigers of Tamil Eelam

Short Answer Type Questions

1. Mention the causes of conflict between India and Pakistan.

2. Explain the relationship between India and Bhutan.

3. Write a short note on water dispute between India and Bangladesh.

4. What kind of relationship India has with Maldives?

5. Analyse the two political developments of 1940s that led to decision for the creation of Pakistan.

6. What is Indus River Water Treaty? Mention its significance also.

Long Answer Type Questions

1. Describe India's relationship with Pakistan in context of recent developments.

2. What are the contentious issues between India and Bangladesh?

3. Write a brief account of India's relationship with Sri Lanka.

4. What are the common problems of South Asian Countries? Elaborate.

5. Explain the factors responsible for Pakistan's failure in building a stable democracy.

Answer

1. *(c)*   **2.** *(c)*   **3.** *(bd*   **4.** *(b)*   **5.** *(d)*

CHAPTER 03

Globalisation

In this Chapter...

- Meaning of Globalisation
- Debates on Globalisation
- Economic and Political
- India and Globalisation

Meaning of Globalisation

Globalisation refers to the **flow of ideas**, **capital**, **commodities** and **people** across different parts of the world. It leads to worldwide interconnectedness that is created and sustained as an outcome of these constant flows.

The impact of globalisation is uneven as it is not based on general conclusions within different societies. Every society is impacted in a different manner like some societies are impacted more than others.

Causes of Globalisation

- **Technological Factors** It is the most prominent cause of globalisation. Invention of printing, microchips, telephone and internet has revolutionised communication between different parts of the world.

- **Communication** Due to faster means of communication and transport, ideas, commodities and capital move easily to any part of the world.

- **Global Interconnectedness** It is the most important aspect of globalisation because globalisation has not emerged only because of availability of improved communications.
  For example, the bird flu or tsumani cannot be confined to any particular nation. In a similar way, the impact of major economic events is felt outside their immediate local, national or regional environment at a global level.

Manifestations of Globalisation

The manifestations of globalisation include the spatial reorganisation of production, the interpenetration of industries across borders, the spread of financial markets, the diffusion of identical consumer goods to distant countries, massive transfers of population-mainly within the South as well as from the South and the East to the West and an emerging worldwide (though not universal) preference for democracy.

Globalisation provides new dimensions for wider markets, the possibility of producing and marketing a larger range of goods, increasing chances for attracting capitals and access to high technologies. Globalisation is a multi-dimensional concept having **political**, **economic** and **cultural** manifestations.

Political, economic and cultural manifestations are discussed below

Political Manifestations

One of the debates that has arisen as a result of current globalisation processes refer to its continued political impact. Some of the discussions related to it are given below

- Globalisation results in decline of state capacity that is the ability of the government to perform tasks gets reduced. Globalisation has impacted the way the state functions.

- It has set international standards that have be to adhered to in order to keep up with the wave of economic growth through assistance from organisations such as the World Bank and IMF.

- The old 'welfare state' is now giving way to the political philosophy of minimum interference in which state performs certain core functions such as maintenance of law and order and the security of its citizens.
- Sometimes, welfare functions directed at economic and social well-being are withdrawn by the state due to globalisation.
- Market becomes a prime determinant to settle down social and economic priorities in place of welfare.
- The increased role of MNC all over the world leads to a reduction in the capacity of governments to take decisions on their own.
- In a positive manner, state capacity has also received a boost as a consequence of globalisation, with enhanced technologies available at the disposal of the state to collect information about its citizens.

Economic Manifestations

The economic aspects of globalisation is known, as the factor that determines a substantial part of content and direction of current globalisation manifestations that are as follows

- Globalisation involves greater economic flows among various countries of the world.
- It has enhanced trade in commodities among different countries of the world.
- Economic globalisation draws our attention to the role of international institutions like IMF and WTO in determining economic policies across the world.
- Greater economic flows among different countries of the world are usually promoted through economic globalisation. Some of this is voluntary and some forced by international institutions and powerful countries. This flow or exchange can take various forms i.e. commodities, capital, people and ideas.
- The restrictions on the imports and movements of capital have also been reduced which facilitates free flow of trade. It means that investors in the rich countries can invest their money in countries other than their own including developing countries.
- It has also led to the flow of ideas across national boundaries like the spread of internet and computer-related services.
- Globalisation hasn't led to increase in the movement of people especially in the developed countries which guarded their borders with visa policies to ensure the job security of their own citizens.
- While globalisation has led to similar economic policies adopted by governments in different parts of the world, this has generated vastly different outcomes in different parts of the world .
- Economic globalisation has created an intense division of opinion all over the world.

Cultural Manifestations

It refers to the impact of globalisation in what we eat, wear, drink and think. The cultural effect of globalisation poses a threat to different cultures in the world other than Western culture. The cultural manifestations of globalisation consist of two concepts. These are

(i) **Cultural Homogenisation** It is an important aspect of cultural globalisation. It refers to the rise of uniform culture or different cultural practices into one common culture. Although, rise of a uniform culture is not the emergence of a global culture.

   For instance, the popularity of American culture like McDonalds, blue jeans and Hollywood movies has been dominant across the globe. It somehow leads to the shrinking of the rich cultural heritage of the entire globe.

   But cultural manifestations of globalisation are not always negative in nature as sometimes external culture influences simply enlarge our choices and sometimes they modify our culture without posing any real challenge. Like for example burger is not a substitute for a masala dosa.

(ii) **Cultural Heterogenisation** Cultural homogenisation is an aspect of globalisation which also generates an opposite effect. The process leads to each culture becoming more different and distinctive in nature. This phenomenon is defined as cultural heterogenisation.

Debates on Globalisation: Economic and Political Aspects

Economic Aspects

Economic globalisation has led to different opinions across the world. Some of them are discussed below

Critics of Economic Globalisation

- They believe that it is likely to benefit only small section of the population while impoverishing those who are dependent on the government for jobs and welfare.
- They have emphasised the need to ensure institutional safeguards or creating 'social safety nets', to minimise the negative effects of globalisation on those who are economically weak.
- Many movements all over the world feel that safety nets are insufficient or unworkable and called for halt to forced economic globalisation.
- Some economists have described economic globalisation as re-colonisation of the world.

Advocates of Economic Globalisation

- They argue that it generates greater economic growth and well-being for larger sections of the population when there is de-regulation.
- They emphasised that greater trade among countries allows each economy to do what it does best.

- They also argue that economic globalisation is inevitable and it is not wise to resist the history and it provides a challenge that can be responded intelligently without accepting it uncritically.

Political Aspects

Some scholars believed that globalisation is now a forceful process that is unlikely to be reversed. Developing countries and their ability to influence prevailing world trends is rather limited in approach. The challenge for these countries and regions is therefore to find their own responses to the overall trends of globalisation.

In spite of differences between Western and the other countries of the world, there are convincing arguments that call each region of the world to be involved in a broad and deep debate on the behaviour of present globalising world and to design a strategy on how to cope up with the challenges of globalisation.

Some scholars held that government in developing countries need to establish rules that include openness, transparency and credibility in government action as well as absence of bureaucratic interference, discretionary regulations and corruption. Introduction of these mechanisms will help in efficient functioning of market forces. This would also reduce the perception of risk and thereby help to attract investments.

India and Globalisation

- Globalisation has occurred in different parts of the world at different times in history. Flows of wealth, commodities, ideas and people can be traced back several countries in Indian history.
- Globalisation has affected India economically, socially and culturally. India removed restrictions on imports of goods after adopting **New Economic Policy** in 1991; which also boosted the investes to invest in India.
- Foreign Direct Investment has increased the production of goods and services and it has also enhanced foreign exchange reserves.
- The European and USA culture spreaded in India after adoption of globalisation which bring about changes in food habits and dressing style.
- Families are converting from joint to nuclear.
- Information technology and space technology have been enhanced after globalisation.
- India have been also participating in trade and commerce with other nations. India plays a leadership role at many other places.

However, in India resistance to globalisation has come from various quaters like Trade Unions of industrial work force and through social movements.

There have been left-wing protests to economic liberalisation voiced through political parties as well as through forums like Indian Social Forum.

While it is too early to assess how beneficial this has been for India, the final test is ensuring that the advantages of progress are shared so that everyone benefits.

Chapter Practice

Objective Questions

• Multiple Choice Questions

1. What do you mean by globalisation?
(a) Flow of ideas
(b) Capital
(c) Commodities and people across the world
(d) All of the above

Ans. (d) Globalisation refers to the flow of ideas, capital, commodities and people across different parts of the world.

2. The process of integration of different countries is called as ....
(a) Privatisation   (b) Globalisation
(c) Liberalisation   (d) None of these

Ans. (b) The process of integration of different countries is called as globalisation. It leads to world wide interconnectedness through which different countries interact with each other.

3. Which of the statements are true about globalisation?
(i) Globalisation is purely an economic phenomenon.
(ii) Globalisation began in 1991.
(iii) Globalisation is the same thing as westernisation.
(iv) Globalisation is a multi-dimensional phenomenon.
Codes
(a) Both (i) and (ii)
(b) Both (iii) and (iv)
(c) Only (iv)
(d) Only (i)

Ans. (c) The statement true about globalisation is that it is a multi-dimensional phenomenon. Globalisation refers to the growing influence exerted at local, national and regional level by financial, economic, environmental, political, social and cultural processes that are global in scope.

4. Which of the statements are true about the causes of globalisation?
(a) Technology is an important cause of globalisation.
(b) Globalisation is caused by a particular community of people.
(c) Globalisation originated in the US.
(d) Economic interdependence alone causes globalisation.

Ans. (a) Technology is an important cause of globalisation. The invention of telegraph, telephone, microchips has revolutionised communication between different parts of the world.

5. Contemporary globalisation points out that it is the .... and ...... of these flows that account for the uniqueness of globalisation in the contemporary era.
(a) value and need
(b) money and market
(c) scale and speed
(d) quantity and quality

Ans. (c) Contemporary globalisation points out that it is the scale and speed of these flows that accounts for the uniqueness of globalisation in the contemporary era.

6. Which of the following is/are true about cultural Homogenisation?
(a) It refers to the rise of uniform culture of different cultural practices into one common culture.
(b) It is an important aspect of globalisation.
(c) It is viewed negatively as it leads to reduction in cultural diversity.
(d) All of the above

Ans. (d) Cultural homogenisation is an important aspect of globalisation. It refers to the rise of uniform culture or different cultural practices into one common culture. It is viewed negatively as it leads to shrinking of rich cultural heritage of entire globe.

7. Which of the following statement(s) is/are correct about economic manifestations?
(i) It has created on intense division of opinion all over the world.
(ii) The primary status remains unchallenged on the basis of political community.
(iii) It is likely to benefit small section of population.
Codes
(a) Only (i)   (b) both (ii) and (iii)
(c) Both (i) and (ii)   (d) Only (iii)

Ans. (c) Statement (i) and (ii) are correct about economic manifestation of globalisation as it has created an on intense division of opinion all over the world and the primary status remains unchallenged on basis of political community.

8. Consider the following statement(s) that have contributed to the process of globalisation. Choose the correct statement(s).
(a) Liberalisation and privatisation
(b) Technological innovations
(c) Role of international organisations such as IMF and WTO
(d) All of the above

Ans. (d) Liberalisation and privatisation, technological innovations and role of international organisations such as IMF and WTO have contributed to the process of globalisation.

9. Choose the correct option that has significantly contributed to the process of Globalisation.
(a) Fear of War
(b) Security Threats
(c) Advancement of Technology
(d) Achievements of the United Nations

Ans. (c) Advancement of Technology has significantly contributed to the process of globalisation.

10. Which of the statements arc true about the impact of globalisation?
(i) Globalisation has been uneven in its impact on states and societies.
(ii) Globalisation has had a uniform impact on all states and societies.
(iii) The impact of globalisation has been confined to the political sphere.
(iv) Globalisation inevitably results in cultural homogeneity.
Codes
(a) Both (i) and (iv)   (b) Both (ii) and (iii)
(c) Both (i) and (ii)   (d) Both (iii) and (iv)

Ans. (a) The impact of globalisation are
• It has been uneven on states and societies creating class and castes.
• It has inevitably resulted in cultural homogeneity.

11. Critics of globalisation argue that globalisation will result in ....
(a) Cultural homogenisation   (b) Cultural heterogenisation
(c) Greater economic growth   (d) Greater economic disparity

Ans. (d) Critics of globalisation argue that globalisation will result in greater economic disparity.

12. Due to globalisation, culture of a country becomes more diverse and distinctive, this process is called ....
(a) cultural complexity
(b) cultural diversity
(c) cultural homogenisation
(d) cultural heterogenisation

Ans. (d) Due to globalisation, culture of a country becomes more diverse and distinctive, this process is called as cultural heterogenisation.

13. Trade unions is related to ....
(a) industrial workforce   (b) agricultural labourers
(c) politicians   (d) government employees

Ans. (a) Trade unions is related to the industrial workforce. It an organised association of workers in a trade, profession formed to protect their interest and rights.

14. Study the following picture and answer the question.

Which of the following best describes the cartoon?
(a) Strong Military Departments
(b) Invading new markets
(c) US Hegemony
(d) Plight of poor people

Ans. (b) The cartoon best depicts the invading new markets. It was sketched by Andy Singer. Globalisation affects us in our home, in what we eat, drink, wear and indeed in what we think.

15. Study the following picture and answer the question

The cartoon depicts which of the following consequences of globalisation?
(a) Political   (b) Economic
(c) Cultural   (d) Moral

Ans. (b) The cartoon depicts the economic consequences of globalisation. Consumers have access to a wider variety of goods and products and can make choices among variety of products according to their needs and choices.

• Assertion/Reasoning MCQs

Directions (Q. Nos. 16-20) In the questions given below, there are two statements marked as Assertion (A) and Reason (R). Read the statements and choose the correct option.

Codes
(a) Both (A) and (R) are true and (R) is the correct explanation of (A).
(b) Both (A) and (R) are true, but (R) is not the correct explanation of (A).
(c) (A) is true, but (R) is false.
(d) (A) is false, but (R) is true.

16. **Assertion** (A) Globalisation need not always be positive; it can have negative consequences for the people.

Reason (R) Globalisation is a multi-dimensional concept. It has political, economic and cultural manifestations and these must be adequately distinguished.

Ans. (b) Both A and R are true, but R is not the correct explanation of A as globalisation can be both positive and negative depending upon person to person and country to country. Globalisation is a multi-dimensional concept as movement of capital takes place from one destination to another, people move in search of better jobs, commodities are transferred and traded across countries etc.

17. **Assertion** (A) While globalisation is not caused by any single factor, technology remains a critical element.

Reason (R) The ability of ideas, capital, commodities and people to move more easily from one part of the world to another has been made possible largely by technological advances.

Ans. (a) Both A and R are true and R is the correct explanation of A. The technological revolution has reached around the world with important consequences for business, government and labour market. Computer aided designs, telecommunication etc are allowing small players to complete with traditional giants.

18. **Assertion** (A) Globalisation results in an erosion of state capacity, that is, the ability of government to do what they do.

Reason (R) Globalisation also gives freedom to governments to act in an arbitrary manner as far as the global issues are concerned.

Ans. (c) A is true as all over the world the old welfare state is now giving way to more minimalist state that performs certain core functions.

R is false as globalisation has put several restrains on government by inducing pressure such as withdrawing economic aid, doing away with transfers and subsidies etc.

19. **Assertion** (A) The critics argue that contemporary globalisation represents a particular phase of global capitalism that makes the rich richer (and fewer) and the poor poorer.

Reason (R) Weakening of the state leads to a reduction in the capacity of the state to protect the interest of its poor.

Ans. (a) Both A and R are true and R is the correct explanation of A as globalisation leads to an increase in income inequality which in turn encourages prosperous nations to outsource production to location which provide either cheap labour or cheap raw materials.

20. **Assertion** (A) There have been left wing protests to economic liberalisation voiced through political parties as well as through forums like the Indian Social Forum.

Reason (R) The left wing believed that globalisation would corrupt the politics of India.

Ans. (c) A is true as resistance to globalisation in India has come from different quarters. The left wing of India criticised globalisation mainly on the issue of the entries of multinational companies and foreign investment that would corrupt the politics of India.

• Cased Based MCQs

1. Read the following and answer the questions.

At the most simple level, globalisation results in an erosion of state capacity that is, the ability of government to do what they do. All over the world, the old 'welfare state' is now giving way to a more minimalist state that performs certain core functions such as the maintenance of law and order and the security of its economic and social well-being. In place of the welfare state, it is the market that becomes the prime determinant of economic and social priorities.

(i) Erosion of state here means ....
(a) Reduction in the role of state in society and economy.
(b) Welfare state is being promoted in the society.
(c) Market economy is being prevalent in the society.
(d) None of the above

Ans. (a) Erosion of state here means reduction in the role of state in society and economy.

(ii) Why is the concept of welfare state giving way to a minimalist state?

(a) As it performs according to the free market economy norms.

(b) As it performs only crucial functions like maintenance of law.

(c) As it is not providing welfare services to the poor people.

(d) All of the above

Ans. (b) The concept of welfare state giving way to a minimalist state is because it performs only crucial function like maintenance of law.

(iii) How has the market become the prime determinant of social priorities?

(a) State is making decision on the basis of market forces.

(b) Market is the prime determinant which influences the role of state.

(c) Market has been forcing the state in the decision-making process for the society.

(d) All of the above

Ans. (d) The market has become the prime determinant of social priorities as the state makes decision on the basis of market forces, market being the prime determinant influences the role of state and has been forcing the state in decision-making process.

(iv) Which of the following are the functions of welfare state?

(a) To provide subsidies to the poor.

(b) To make welfare policies for the poor.

(c) To make policies for the benefit of private sector.

(d) Both (a) and (b)

Ans. (d) The functions of welfare state are

- To provide subsidies to poor.
- To make welfare policies for poor.

PART 2

Subjective Questions

• Short Answer Type Questions

1. Define globalisation. How is it different from internationalisation? **[All India 2011]**

Ans. Globalisation refers to the flow of ideas, capital, commodities and people across different parts of the world. It is different from internationalisation on the basis of following points

- Internationalisation believes in the integrity of community, whereas globalisation believes in one umbrella concept and sharing of ideas between other states.
- Internationalisation believes in the use of resources of all the world equally for the benefit of mankind, but globalisation emphasise on the development of resources for the welfare and support of community.

- Internationalisation also believes in the universal brotherhood and international peace, whereas globalisation believes in the concept of flow of ideas, people and commodities throughtout the globe. It also encourages the richer countries to support the poorer countries' economy.

2. Explain any two major causes of globalisation. **[Delhi 2019]**

Ans. Two major causes of globalisation are

(i) Technology is the most important element. The invention of the telegraph, the telephone and the microchip has revolutionised communication between various global factors. The technology has made it easier to exchange ideas, capital and commodities from one place to another. The transfer of capital and commodities is a major cause of globalisation.

(ii) The increased interconnectedness has led to migration of people in search of economic opportunities. This in turn helps in the flow of investments across the world. This has initiated globalisation on a large scale.

3. What are the political consequences of globalisation?

or Mention any two political consequences of globalisation. **[Delhi 2012]**

Ans. Following are the consequences of political globalisation

- It has eroded the capacity of the state by reducing the ability of the government to do what they want.
- The concept of welfare state has been reduced to a more minimalist state all over the world.
- Market becomes a prime determinant to settle down social and economic priorities is place of welfare.
- The increased role of MNC all over the world leads to a reduction in the capacity of governments to take decisions on their own.

4. How has technology contributed to globalisation? Explain. **[NCERT, Delhi 2013; All India 2009]**

Ans. Technology has contributed to globalisation in the folowing ways

- The technological inventions such as telegraph, telephone and the microchip has revolutionised communication between various global factors and hence invention of printing laid the basis for the emergence of nationalism. Thus, technology influences the way we think of our personal and collective lives. The sharing of ideas, capital, commodities and people throughout the globe has been made possible only by technological advancement.
- The transfer of capital goods and services is likely to be wider and quicker than the transfer of people across the various parts of the world.
- Technological advances has reduced the physical distances and increased interconnectedness worldwide.

5. What are the economic manifestations of globalisation? **[Delhi 2009]**

Ans. Following are the economic manifestations of globalisation

- It deals with increasing the trade in commodities all around the world. The restrictions imposed by various states on each other's imports have been removed.
- Globalisation benefits some sections of society, while other sections of society are left deprived. Developed countries gain more as compared to developing countries.
- Greater economic flows among different countries of the world are usually promoted through economic globalisation. This flow or exchange can take various forms i.e. commodities, capital, people and ideas.
- The restrictions on the imports and movements of capital have also been reduced which facilitates free flow of trade. It means that investors in the rich countries can invest their money in countries other than their own including developing countries.

6. Explain any two positive and any two negative effects of globalisation. **[All India 2014]**

Ans. Positive impacts of globalisation are *(any two)*

  (i) Increase in the volume of trade in goods and services.

  (ii) It attracts private foreign capital investment.

  (iii) It creates new job opportunities.

  (iv) It raises standard of living.

  (v) It increases production, efficiency and healthy competition.

  (iv) It attracts foreign direct investment also.

Negative impacts of globalisation are *(any two)*

  (i) The foreign companies focus on their profit orientation projects only in place of social welfare.

  (ii) It has widened income disparities by making the rich more richer and the poor more poorer.

  (iii) Globalisation is also a reason for depletion of flora and fauna in country.

7. Critically evaluate the impact of the changing role of the state in the developing countries in the light of globalisation.

Ans. The impact of the changing role of the state in the developing countries in the light of globalisation is discussed below

- State only plays a minimal role which includes core functions like maintenance of law and order as well as security.
- Globalisation has further restricted the role of state as it minimise the role of state in the economy. It reduces the State capacity and it is being completely dominated by the market forces.
- The position of state has also been relieved due to globalisation as it increases technological developments which help the state to run efficiently.

- Globalisation has impacted the way the state functions and set international standards that have to be adhered in order to keep up with the wave of economic growth through assistance from organisations such as World Bank and IMF.
- However, the state has become more transparent and even though they are answerable to other governing bodies, the state still has influence.

8. Do you agree with the argument that globalisation leads to cultural heterogeneity? **[NCERT]**

Ans. No, globalisation leads to both cultural homogenisation and cultural heterogenisation as

- Though cultural homogenisation is an arena of globalisation, the same process generates the opposite effect also prompts each culture resulting into cultural heterogenisation where each become more different and distinct.
- Globalisation leads to the rise of uniform culture known as cultural homogenisation i.e. the influence of Western culture.
- The difference among powers remain the same despite the exchange of culture. Hence, it may be said that cultural exchange is only one of many processes.

9. Describe effects of globalisation on the economy of a country. **[All India 2015]**

Ans. Following are the three effects of globalisation on the economy of a country *(any three)*

  (i) Economic globalisation gives more importance to institutions like the IMF and the WTO and their role in determining economic policies across world.

  (ii) It involves greater economic flows among different countries of the world in which some of them are forced by international institutions and powerful countries.

  (iii) As the restrictions imposed by different countries have been reduced, so greater trade in commodities across the globe can be seen.

  (iv) Globalisation has led to similar economic policies adopted by governments in different parts of the world, this has generated vastly different outcomes in different parts of the world.

  (v) Economic globalisation has also brought economic ruin for the weaker countries, especially for the poor within these countries.

10. "Globalisation has shifted power from nation-states to global consumers." Justify the statement. **[All India 2012]**

Ans. Globalisation has shifted power from nation-states to global consumers because of the following points:

- Revolution in information technology and electronic media and development in the field of science and technology.
- Collapse of communism and the end of Cold War with the disintegration of Soviet Union.

- Advances in the field of transport and communication and growth of MNCs. These MNCs are the efforts of the developed nations to make the whole world as one single market.
- Rising debts of developing states that have forced the IMF and World Bank to ask developing states to adopt the path of disinvestment and globalisation.

11. Explain any three benefits of globalisation with examples. **[Delhi 2014]**

Ans. The three benefits of globalisation are as follows

  (i) **Economic Benefits**

    (a) It involves greater economic flows among various countries.

    (b) It has enhanced trade in commodities among countries.

    (c) The restrictions on the imports and movement of capital have also been reduced.

    (d) This has spread internet and computer related services across national boundaries.

  (ii) **Technological Benefits**

    (a) Technological equipments as telephone, internet, telegraph and microchip have contributed to globalisation.

    (b) This is by exchanging ideas, capitals and people to make convenient to move from one place to another at a fast pace to stimulate the process of globalisation.

  (iii) **Political Benefits**

    (a) The primary status remains unchallenged on the basis of political community.

    (b) States have received a boost under globalisation to become more powerful and strong.

• Long Answer Type Questions

1. What is worldwide interconnectedness? What are its components? **[NCERT]**

Ans. Globalisation is defined as worldwide interconnectedness. Globalisation fundamentally means the flow of ideas, capital, commodities and people across different parts of the world.

The crucial element is the 'worldwide interconnectedness', that is created and sustained as a consequence of these constant flows. It is a multi-dimensional concept as it has political, economic and cultural manifestations and these must be adequately distinguished. The impact of globalisation is vastly uneven because it affects some societies more than others and some parts of some societies more than others.

The major components of worldwide interconnectedness i.e. globalisation are:

Technological Advancement Technology remains an important factor with regard to globalisatioin. The technological inventions such as telegraph, telephone and

the microchip has revolutionised communication between various global factors.

Thus, technological advancements has been most significant component of worldwide interconnectedness.

Free Flow of Capital and Investment It has also been the key component of rising worldwide interconnectedness. Flow of FDI across the world has transform the world into a interconnected global market.

Migration and Movement of People It has also been responsible for growing worldwide interconnectedness. Technological advancement has reduced the physical distances and increased the migration and movement of people from one country to another.

Sharing of Ideas and Knowledge It has also been responsible for increasing interconnectedness. With technological advancement, ideas and knowledge are rapidly moving from one part to another parts of world.

2. Write down the features of Globalisation in detail.

Ans. Some of the important features of Globalisation are discussed below

  (i) **Rapid Expansion of International Trade** Globalisation involves free flow of trade across the globe. World Trade Organisation is an example of or expansion of trade across countries. WTO's purpose is to enlarge production and trade of services to ensure optimum utilisation of world resources and to facilitate international trade.

  (ii) **Growing Importance of MNC's** Multinational Corporations are necessary for understanding globalisation. MNC's produce market services in countries other than their enhancing profit in the Global Market.

  (iii) **Increase in Technological Inventions** Globalisation has led to increase in technological inventions which has enhanced interconnectedness across the globe. The inventions of telegraph, telephone and the microchip in more recent times has revolutionised communication between different parts of the world.

  (iv) **Increase in Capital Transfer** Flow of capital across the globe increases economic cooperation among the nations. In operational terms, it means that investors in the rich countries can invest their money in rich countries other than their own including developing countries where they might get better returns.

3. Describe any three effects of globalisation on the culture of a country. **[All India 2015]**

  or Evaluate the cultural consequences of globalisation. **[Delhi 2019]**

Ans. The effects of globalisation on the culture of a country are

  (i) Cultural globalisation affects our food, clothes and thinking. But some times, external influence simply enlarge our choices and sometimes they modify our culture without overwhelming the traditional norms. For example, the burger is no substitute for a masala dosa and therefore, does not pose any real challenge.

In the same way, blue jeans can go well with a homespun *Khadi Kurta*. Here the outcome of outside influences is a new combination that is unique. This clothing combination has been exported back to the country that gave us blue jeans.

(ii) The culture of the politically and economically dominant society leave its imprint on a less powerful society, and the world begins to look more like a dominant power it wishes to be.

(iii) This is dangerous not only for the poor countries but for the whole of humanity, as it leads to the shrinking of the rich cultural heritage of the entire globe.

So, we can say that globalisation broadens our cultural outlook and promotes cultural homogenisation.

4. What are the economic implications of globalisation? How has globalisation impacted on India with regard to this particular dimension?

[NCERT]

Ans. The economic implications of globalisation are as follows

- Economic globalisation gives more importance to institutions like the IMF and the WTO.
- It involves greater economic flows among different countries of the world.
- As the restrictions imposed by different countries have been reduced, so greater trade in commodities across the globe can be seen.
- It has led to the flow of ideas across national boundaries through internet and computer.
- Economic globalisation has also brought economic ruin for the weaker countries, especially for the poor within these countries.

Impact on India

Globalisation affected India economically, socially and culturally. After adopting New Economic Policy in 1991, India has removed restrictions on imports of goods. It also encouraged the investors to invest in India. Foreign Direct Investment to produce goods and services has increased, it also enhanced foreign exchange reserves.

India is also involved in trade and commerce with other nations. Even though at some places, India plays a leadership role. However, in India, resistance to globalisation has come from various quarters.

These are as follows

- Trade Unions of industrial workforce as well as social movements and farmer agitation against monopoly. MNCs are also some forms of resistance to globalisation.
- The acquiring of certain plants like *Neem* by American and European firms has also generated widespread opposition in India.

• Case Based Questions

1. Read the passage given below carefully and answer the following questions.

Globalisation affects us in our home, in what we eat, drink, wear and indeed in what we think. It shapes what we think are our preferences. The cultural effect of globalisation leads to the fear that this process poses a threat to cultures in the world. It does so, because globalisation leads to the rise of a uniform culture or what is called cultural homogenisation. The rise of a uniform culture is not the emergence of a global culture. What we have in the name of a global culture is the imposition of Western culture on the rest of the world. But there are some positive aspects of cultural globalisation as well.

(i) How is cultural homogenisation different from cultural Hetcrogenisation?

(ii) "Sometimes external global influences simply enlarge our choices or modify our culture without overwhelming the traditional system". Given three examples to justify the statement.

(iii) In what forms globalisation affects us?

Ans. (i) When globalisation led to rise of a uniform culture then it is called Cultural homogenisation whereas when globalisation leads to culture becoming more different and distinctive then it is called Cultural heterogenisation.

(ii) Sometimes external global influences simply enlarge our choices or modify four culture without overwhelming the traditional system. Three examples to explain the statement are

  (a) Burger is not a substitute of Masala Dosa so therefore it does not pose any real challenge.

  (b) Blue jeans can go well with a Khadi kurta so this also doesn't pose any real challenge to the culture.

  (c) Coca cola and coconut water are simultaneously enjoyed in summers.

(iii) Globalisation is the process of the worlds system that is increasingly interlinked. Nearly all jobs in the secondary and tertiary sectors of employment are linked to the process of globalisation, it has also increased international migration which has resulted in multicultural societies.

2. Read the passage given below carefully and answer the following questions.

Globalisation does not always reduce state capacity. The primacy of the state continues to be unchallenged basis of political community. The old jealousies and rivalries between countries have not ceased to matter in world politics. The state continues to discharge its essential functions (law and order, national security) and consciously withdraws from certain domains from which it wishes to. States continue to be important. Indeed, in some respects state capacity has received a boost as a consequence of globalisation, with enhanced technologies available at the disposal of the state to collect information about its citizens.

(i) What are the essential functions of the state?

(ii) How do enhanced technologies enable the state to rule better?

(iii) How has globalisation given boost to the state capacity?

Ans. (i) The essential functions of the state are

    (a) To defend and secure the boundaries of the state to maintain national security.

    (b) To provide justice and maintain law and order.

(iii) Enhanced technologies enable the state a rule better as

    (a) The state can collect important information about its citizens.

    (b) State can keep surveillance on its people.

(iii) Globalisation has given boost to the state capacity by providing advance technology to the state to rule its people better.

3. Consider the picture given below and answer the questions that follow.

(i) What are the manifestation of globalisation?

(ii) So many Nepalese workers come to India to work. Is that globalisation?

(iii) Why do farmers commit suicide?

Ans. (i) Globalisation consists of political, economic and cultural manifestations.

(ii) Yes, coming of Nepalese workers to India is a kind of globalisation. They come to India for better livelihood. However, religious bonds seen between nationals of India and Nepal would not exist in globalisation.

(iii) There are various reasons for the suicide of farmers, but the foremost is the debt trap in which they are engulfed by purchasing various inputs from MNCs, such as seeds, fertilizers, etc.

4. Consider the cartoon given below and answer the questions that follow.

(i) On what does the cartoon comment?

(ii) What is referred under the title 'Yesterday' and what is the message conveyed by the title 'Today'?

(iii) What does the cartoon depicts?

Ans. (i) The cartoon comments on the changing scenario due to globalisation.

(ii) It refer under the title 'Yesterday' about the earlier conditions of developing countries who were starving due to less growth in their economy. The title 'convey' that globalisation opened the doors for new entrants from developing nations and resulted into brain drain.

(iii) The cartoon depicts the economic consequences of globalisation. The flow of people to other countries may take away the jobs of citizens of those countries.

Chapter Test

Objective Type Questions

1. Which of the following is incorrect about globalisation?
- (a) Globalisation will result in greater economic growth
- (b) Globalisation will result in greater economic disparity
- (c) Globalisation will result in cultural homogenisation according to some critics
- (d) All of the above

2. Globalisation is a multi-dimensional concept having manifestations like ....
- (a) Political
- (b) Economic
- (c) Cultural
- (d) All of these

3. Due to globalisation, culture of a country becomes more diverse and distinctive, this process is called ....
- (a) cultural complexity
- (b) cultural diversity
- (c) cultural homogenisation
- (d) cultural heterogenisation

4. Consider the following statement which is/are incorrect about the positive effect of globalisation?
- (a) It has widened income disparity.
- (b) It is also the reason for depletion of flora and foura.
- (c) It has attracted private foreign capital investment.
- (d) Both (a) and (b)

5. The negative impact of globalisation .... to generate sufficient employment.
- (a) increased
- (b) decreased
- (c) failed
- (d) None of these

Short Answer Type Questions

1. How does globalisation leads to cultural homogenisation?

2. Globalisation leads to cultural heterogenisation. Explain.

3. Explain the causes of globalisation.

4. What are the economic manifestations of globalisation?

5. How have technological advancement and recognition of interconnectedness affected globalisation?

6. Give examples to show that globalisation has affected our food habits.

Long Answer Type Questions

1. Discuss the economic implications of globalisation.

2. How has technology contributed to globalisation?

3. What are the positive and negative effects of globalisation?

4. "Globalisation has shifted power from nation-states to global consumers." Justify the statements.

5. Explain political consequences of globalisation.

Answers

1. *(a)*   **2.** *(d)*   **3.** *(c)*   **4.** *(d)*   **5.** *(c)*

PART B
Politics in India Since Independence

1. Parties and the Party Systems in India
2. Democratic Resurgence
3. Indian Politics : Trends and Developments

Parties and the Party Systems in India

In this Chapter...

- Challenge of Building Democracy
- First General Election
- Congress Dominance in the First Three General Elections
- Political Parties and their Functions
- Emergence of Opposition Parties
- Party System
- Party System in India

Challenge of Building Democracy

India faced the serious challenge of nation-building in the beginning. India's national unity was first priority of its leaders. They thought democracy will introduce differences and conflicts. Other such countries that got freedom from colonialism have witnessed non-democratic government in form of nominal democracy, one-party rule or direct army rule. In India, every society has different groups with different conflicting aspirations and needs. To resolve these differences, India decided to take the path of democracy.

Formation of Election Commission

Indian Constitution came into effect on 26th January, 1950 but that time the country was being governed by an **interim government**. The Election Commission of India was set up in January 1950. **Sukumar Sen** has been appointed as the **first Chief Election Commissioner**.

Problems Faced by Election Commission

For holding free and fair election in a country, the Election Commission faced following problems

- Holding an election required delimitation or drawing the boundaries of the electoral constituencies. It also required preparing the electoral rolls, or the list of all the citizens eligible to vote.
- Only 15 per cent of eligible voters were literate.
- The vast size of country was a big challenge.

In this context, India's experiment with **Universal Adult Franchise**[1] appeared very bold and risky.

First General Election

First general election was held from October, 1951 to February 1952. But this election was referred as the 1952 election because most parts of the country voted in January 1952. It took six months for campaigning, polling and counting to be completed.

Elections were competitive as there were on an average more than four candidates for each seat. The results were accepted as fair even by the losers. India's general election of 1952 became a landmark in the history of democracy all over the world. It proved that democracy could be practised anywhere in the world.

In the first general election of 1952, Congress party won 364 seats out of 489 seats, and finished far ahead of any other challenger. The **Communist Party of India** came next in terms

---

1. **Universal Adult Franchise** All adults who are citizens of a country and are above 18 years of age are allowed to vote irrespective of their social and economic back.

of seats and won only 16 seats. State elections were also held with the Lok Sabha elections.

Congress scored big victory in state elections as well. It won a majority of seats in all the states except **Travancore-Cochin, Madras** and **Odisha**. Thus, the Congress party ruled all over the country at the national and state level.

The Congress maintained the same position in second and third general election held in 1957 and 1962 respectively. It won three-fourth of Lok Sabha seats. No opposition parties could win even one-tenth of the number of seats won by Congress.

The Congress won three out of every four seats, but it did not get even half of the votes. In this system of election, the party that gets more votes than others tends to get much more than its proportional share.

Changing Methods of Voting

These days we use an Electronic Voting Machine (EVM) to record voters' preferences. In the first general election, it was decided to place inside each polling booth a box for each candidate with the election symbol of that candidate.

Each voter was given a blank ballot paper which they had to drop into the box of the candidate they wanted to vote for.

After the first two elections this method was changed. Now the ballot paper carried the names and symbols of all the candidates and the voter was required to put a stamp on the name of the candidate they wanted to vote for. Towards the end of 1990s the Election Commission started using the EVM. By 2004, the entire country had shifted to the EVM.

Congress Dominance in the First Three General Elections

The result of the first general election did not surprise anyone. The Indian National Congress was expected to win this election. Congress evolved from its origin in 1885 as a pressure group of newly educated, professional and commercial class to a mass movement in the 20th century. It was the only party having an organisation and having most popular leader like **Jawaharlal Nehru.**

- The legacy of the freedom movement was an important reason of Congress dominance in General Election.

- Congress was very well organised and had organisational presence across India along with organisational network to the local.

- Its inclusive nature made it popular among all sections of society.

- Thus, all these factors led to the dominance of Congress Party. However, in the first decade of electoral competition, the Congress acted both as the ruling party as well as the opposition. Therefore, this period of Indian politics has been called as the Congress System.

Congress as Social and Ideological Coalition

At the time of independence, the Congress became a social coalition representing the India's diversity in terms of class, castes, religion and language. Many of these groups either merged their identity within the Congress or continued to exist within the Congress holding different beliefs. Thus, Congress became an ideological coalition as well.

Tolerance and Management of Factions

The coalition-like character of Congress made it stronger and inclusive in the following ways

- A coalition accommodates all those who are part of it and strike a balance on almost all issues. Compromise and inclusiveness are the basic characteristics of a coalition. This strategy made opposition difficult to be developed because all issues and concerns find a place in the programme and ideology of the Congress.

- Coalition nature of Congress developed a greater tolerance of internal differences and accommodated the needs and aspirations of various groups and leaders. Congress did both these things during the freedom struggle and continued doing this even after independence.

If a group was not satisfied with the position of the party, they remain inside the party and fight the other groups rather than leaving the party and becoming an 'opposition'.

Such a group inside the party are called **factions**. Instead of being a weakness, factionalism became strength of the Congress. The system of factions functioned as a balancing mechanism within the ruling party.

Unique Phase of Indian Politics

The first phase of democratic politics in our country was quite unique. There was a lot of mutual respect between the leaders of the Congress and of the opposition. The interim government formed after the declaration of independence and first general election even included the opposition leaders like Ambedkar and Shyama Prasad Mukherjee in the cabinet.

Socialist leaders like **Jayprakash Narayan** was also invited to join government by Nehru. This kind of personal relationship and respect for political adversaries started declining when competition between parties become more intense. The key role of the Congress in the freedom struggles gave it edge over other political parties. But with the passage of time when congress ability to accommodate all interests and aspirants for political power started declining, other political parties started becoming more popular. Thus, domination of Congress lasted only one phase in the politics of India.

Political Parties and their Functions

A political party is a group of people who come together to contest elections and hold power in the government. They agree on some policies and programmes for the society with a view to promote the collective good.

The main functions of political parties are discussed below

- **Contesting Elections** Political parties contest elections by nominating its candidate for the electoral contest in various constituencies.
- **Policies and Programmes** Political parties put forward different policies and programmes so that the voters can choose from them.
- **Making Law** Political parties play a decisive role in making laws for the country. Most of the parliamentarians belong to political parties, so a political party has direct say in law making of the country.
- **Formation of Government** Political parties form and run governments. The executive body is formed by people from the ruling party.
- **Playing Opposition** A party which does not get majority or come under the majority coalition, needs to play the role of opposition. It keeps an eye on the ruling government, criticises them and mobilises opposition to ruling party.
- **Shaping Public Opinion** Political parties shape public opinion. They do so by raising and highlighting issues in the legislature and in the media.
- **Providing Access to Government Machinery** Political parties provide people access to government machinery and welfare schemes implemented by governments. Parties need to be responsive to people's needs and demands.

Emergence of Opposition Parties

India had a larger number of diverse and vibrant opposition parties than many other multi-party democracies. Some of these had came into existence even before the first general election of 1952. The root of all the non-Congress parties that exist now be traced to 1950s. All these opposition parties have has only a token representation in the Lok Sabha and State Assemblies, but their presence played a crucial role in maintaining the democratic character of the system.

Role of Opposition Parties

The opposition parties offered a sustained and principled criticism of the policies and practices of the Congress party. They kept the Congress under check and influenced the balance of power within the Congress party. They prevented the anger with system taking anti-democratic path by providing democratic political alternative. They also groomed the leaders who played important role in shaping the future of our country. Some opposition parties are given below

Socialist Party

Socialist Party was formed in 1934 by **Acharya Narendra Dev.** Later on, it was separated to form Socialist Party in 1948 with ideology of democratic socialism and criticised capitalism.

The Socialist Party went through many splits and reunions leading to the formation of many Socialist Parties.

These included the Kisan Mazdoor Praja Party, the Praja Socialist Party and Samyukta Socialist Party. Jayaprakash Narayan, Achyut Patwardhan, Asoka Mehta, Acharya Narendra Dev, Rammanohar Lohia and SM Joshi were among the leaders of the socialist parties. Many parties in contemporary India, like the Samajwadi Party, the Rashtriya Janata Dal, Janata Dal (United) and the Janata Dal (Secular) trace their origins to the Socialist Party.

Bharatiya Jana Sangh

It was formed in 1951 by **Shyama Prasad Mukherjee** with the ideology of one country, one culture and one nation and called for a reunion of India and Pakistan in *Akhand Bharat*. The party was a consistent advocate of India developing nuclear weapons especially after China carried out its atomic tests in 1964.

In the 1950s, Jana Sangh remained on the margins of the electoral politics and was able to secure only 3 Lok Sabha seats in 1952 elections and 4 seats in 1957 general elections to Lok Sabha. In the early years its support came mainly from the urban areas in the Hindi speaking states like Rajasthan, Madhya Pradesh, Delhi and Uttar Pradesh. The party's leaders included Shyama Prasad Mukherjee, Deen Dayal Upadhyaya and Balraj Madhok.

Communist Party of India

In the early 1920, communist groups emerged in different parts of India having a belief of communism. The Communist Party of India was primarily secular, modern and authoritarian. From 1935, the Communists worked mainly from within the fold of the Indian National Congress. A parting of ways took place in December 1941, when the Communists decided to support the British in their war against Nazi Germany.

AK Gopalan, SA Dange, EMS Namboodiripad, PC Joshi, Ajay Ghosh and P Sundarraya were among the notable leaders of the CPI. The party went through a major split in 1964 following the ideological rift between Soviet Union and China. The pro-Soviet faction remained as the CPI, while the opponents formed the CPI(Marxist). Both these parties continue to exist to this day.

Communist Victory in Kerala

In the assembly elections held in March 1957, the Communist Party won the largest number of seats to the Kerala legislature. The party won 60 of the 126 seats and had the support of five independents. The Governor invited **EMS Namboodiripad**, the leader of the Communist legislature party, to form the ministry. For the first time in the world, a Communist party government had come to power through democratic elections. In 1959, the Congress Government at the Centre dismissed the Communist Government in Kerala under Article 356 of the Constitution.

Swatantra Party

Swatantra Party was formed in August 1959 after the Nagpur Resolution of the Congress which called for land ceilings. Its important leaders were C Rajagopalachari, KM Munshi, NG Ranga, and Minoo Masani. Its ideology emphasised on the free economy and less involvement of government in controlling the economy and advocated closer relations with the USA.

The Swatantra Party was against land ceilings in agriculture and opposed co-operative farming and state trading. It was also opposed to the progressive tax regime and demanded dismantling of the licensing regime.

Problems during the 1967 Elections

The year 1967 is regarded as a landmark year in India's electoral and political history. The country during 1967 elections experienced major changes. These are as follows

- Two Prime Ministers had died in quick succession and the new Prime Minister (Indira Gandhi), who had been in office for less than a year was regarded as politically amateur.
- This period was characterised by serious economic crises because of failure of monsoon, widespread drought, decline in agriculture production, food shortage, depletion of foreign exchange reserves, drop in industrial production and exports as well as sharp increase in military expenditure.
- The devaluation of Indian Rupee was also undertaken by Indira government.
- Economic situation caused price rise in the country. People started protesting against the price rise of essential commodities, food shortage, growing unemployment and overall economic conditions in the country.
- The government treated protest, strike, dharna as a law and order problem, not as expressions of the people's problems. This further increased public bitterness and reinforced public dissatisfaction.
- The communist and socialist parties launched struggles for greater equality. Communist Party of India (Marxist-Leninist) led armed agrarian struggles and organised peasant agitations.
- This period also witnessed some of the worst Hindu-Muslim riots since Independence.

Non-Congressism

This situation was also affected from ongoing party politics in the country. Opposition parties were in the forefront of organising public protests and pressurising the government. Non-Congress political parties realised that the division of their votes kept the Congress in power.

The parties that were entirely different and desperate in their ideology and programmes came together to form anti-Congress front in some state and also entered seat sharing arrangement in other. They thought that the inexperience of Indira Gandhi and internal factionalism within the Congress will help them to collapse the Congress. **Ram Mahonar Lohiya,** a socialist leader called this strategy 'non-Congressism'.

Party System

Party system refers to the typical structure of parties within a political system. It describes the number of parties that compete effectively in a political culture. It depends on the nature of society, social and regional diversities. A particular party system takes time to evolve in a country.

There are majorly three types of party systems that are

(i) **One-party System** It refers to a political framework where one or single political party forms and runs the government. For example, in China all powers are vested with the Communist Party of China.

(ii) **Bi-party System** It refers to a political framework where two major parties dominate voting at all levels of government. For example, the United States is an example of a two-party system in which the majority of elected officials are either Democrats or Republicans.

(iii) **Multi-Party System** A multi-party system is where many parties compete for power and government will often pass between coalitions formed by different combinations of parties. India is an example of Multi-party coalition system.

Party System in India

Indian party system is unique in its own way and has always remained vibrant. The vast menu of choices in terms of political leaders or parties makes it flexible in nature. The nature of party system in India is divided into different phases which are discussed below

Bi-party System

The results of the states and general elections of 1967 proved that the Congress could be defeated in the elections. After these elections, Indira Gandhi faced challenged from her own party. A group of powerful and influential leaders within the Congress known as **Syndicate** led by K Kamraj the then President of Congress Party (Former CM of Tamil Nadu). It included powerful state leaders like SK Patil of Bombay city (Now Mumbai), S Nijalingappa of Mysore, (Karnataka) N Sanjeeva Reddy of Andhra Pradesh and Atulya Ghosh of West Bengal. Both Lal Bahadur Shastri and Indira Gandhi owned their position to the support received from the syndicate.

Syndicate group had a decisive say in Indira Gandhi's first Council of Ministers and also in policy formulation and implementation. These leaders expected that Indira Gandhi would follow their advice. But gradually, Indira Gandhi took a strong position within the government and party. She chooses her trusted group of advisors from outside the party and carefully side-lined the Syndicates. This led to the emergence of bi-party system in the Indian party system.

Events Which Influenced the Split of Congress Party

- This split in the Congress party was evident during the 1969 Presidential elections. The post of President fell vacant that year after the death of Zakir Hussain.
- Despite Indira Gandhi's reservations, the Syndicate nominated their opponent and then Speaker of Lok Sabha, N Sanjeeva Reddy, as the official Congress candidate for Presidential elections. Indira Gandhi encourages the then Vice President, VV Giri to stand for Presidential elections as an independent candidate.
- Indira Gandhi also launched ten point programme in which several popular policy measures like nationalisation of 14 leading private banks abolition of Privy Purse, land reforms distribution of food grains, ceiling on urban property and provision of houses to poor were conducted.
- Morarji Desai was the Deputy Prime Minister and Finance Minister. On both issues, serious conflict measures emerged between him and Prime Minister Indira Gandhi due to which he left the government. The then Congress President S Nijalingappa issued a 'whip' asking all the Congress MP's and MLA's to vote in favour of N Sanjeeva Reddy.
- The Congress was divided into two factions, right and left. Left attacked Morarji Desai as the representative of big bussiness houses.
- Indira Gandhi silently supported VV Giri and she publicly called for a conscience vote which meant that the MP's and MLA's from the Congress are free to vote the way they want.
- Finally, the elections resulted in the victory of VV Giri. The defeat of Sanjeeva Reddy, official Congress candidate formalised the split in the party.

After these elections, the Congress President expelled the Prime Minister from the party. Indira Gandhi claimed that her group was the real Congress. By November 1969, group led by Syndicate was called as the Congress (Organisation) and the group led by Indira Gandhi was called the Congress (Requisitionists). These two parties were described as Old Congress and New Congress. Indira Gandhi projected this split as an ideological divide between socialists and conservatives, between pro-poor and pro-rich.

Abolition of Privy Purse

The integration of the Princely States was preceded by an assurance that after the dissolution of princely rule, the then rulers' families would be allowed to retain certain private property and given a grant in heredity or government allowance, measured on the basis of the extent, revenue and potential of the merging state. This grant was called the Privy Purse.

At the time of accession, there was little criticism of these privileges since integration and consolidation was the primary aim. Following the 1967 elections, Indira Gandhi supported the demand that the government should abolish Privy Purses. Morarji Desai, however, called the move morally wrong and amounting to a 'breach of faith with the princes'.

The government tried to bring a Constitutional amendment in 1970, but it was not passed in Rajya Sabha. It then issued an ordinance which was struck down by the Supreme Court. Indira Gandhi made this into a major election issue in 1971 and got a lot of public support. Following its massive victory in the 1971 election, the Constitution was amended to remove legal obstacles for abolition of 'Privy Purse'.

Multi-Party Coalition System

The elections of 1967 brought the phenomenon of multi-party coalitions. As no single party got majority, various non-Congress parties came together to form joint legislative parties that supported non-Congress government i.e. SVD (Samyukt Vidhayak Dal) governments. In most of these cases, the coalition partners were ideologically opposite to each other.

For example, the SVD government in Bihar was formed with coalition of socialist parties SSP (Samyukta Socialist Party) and PSP (Praja Socialist Party) along with CPI on the left and Jana Sangha on the right.

In Punjab, it was called the Popular United Front formed by two rival Akali parties, Sant group and Master group with both communist parties, CPI and CPI (M), SSP, Republican Party and Bhartiya Jana Sangh.

The concept of Alliance politics also emerged after the fifth general elections of 1971, as Congress (R) – CPI alliance won more seats. These votes were far more than Congress ahead ever won in the first four general elections. The Congress (R) and CPI together won 375 seats in the Lok Sabha and secured 48.4% vote share and Indira's Congress (R) itself won 352 seats with 44% vote share.

Contrary to this, Congress (O) with so many strong leaders could win only 16 seats and got less than one-fourth of votes secured by Indira Gandhi's Party. Grand Alliance of the opposition faced a massive failure. They all together won less than 40 seats.

Defection

After the 1967 elections, the important role was played by defections in the making and unmaking of governments in the states. Defection means an elected representatives leaves the party on whose symbol he/she was elected and joins another party. The constant realignment and shifting, political loyalties gave rise to the expression 'Aya Ram, Gaya Rama'. It became popular in India to describe the practice of frequent floor crossing by legislators.

This expression originated when an MLA from Haryana Gaya Lal in 1967 changed his party thrice in a fortnight from Congress to United Front back to Congress and then within nine hours to United Front again. Thus, the Constitution was amended to prevent defections.

Chapter Practice

Objective Questions

• Multiple Choice Questions

1. The Constitution of India was ready and signed on
....

(a) 26th October, 1949   (b) 26th November, 1949
(c) 26th November, 1950   (d) 26th October, 1950

Ans. (b) The Constitution of India was ready and signed on 26th November, 1949. It came into effect on 26th January, 1950.

2. Who was appointed as first Chief Election Commissioner?

(a) Anup Chandra Pandey   (b) Sushil Chandra
(c) Sukumar Sen   (d) Rajiv Kumar

Ans. (c) Sukumar Sen was appointed as first Chief Election Commissioner. The Election Commission of India was set up in January 1950.

3. Which of the following facts about the political parties is incorrect?

(a) They shape public opinion.
(b) They provide people with access to government machinery.
(c) They put forward policies and programmes to attract voters.
(d) They play an active role to resolve public policy problems.

Ans. (d) Political parties don't play an active role to resolve the public policy problems.

4. Which of the following political parties in contemporary India trace their origin to the Socialist Party?

(a) Samyukta Socialist Party
(b) Samajwadi Party
(c) Janta Dal (Secular)
(d) Both (b) and (c)

Ans. (d) Samajwadi Party and Janta Dal (s) political parties trace their origin to the Socialist Party.

5. Bhartiya Jana Sangh was formed in ....

(a) 1950   (b) 1949
(c) 1951   (d) 1952

Ans. (c) Bhartiya Jana Sangh was formed in 1951 that called for reunion of India and Pakistan in Akhand Bharat.

6. Who among the following was the founder of Bhartiya Jana Sangh?

(a) SA Dange
(b) SP Mukherjee
(c) Minoo Masani
(d) Ashok Mehta

Ans. (b) Shyama Prasad Mukherjee founded the Bharatiya Jana Sangh with the ideology of one country, one culture and one nation.

7. Consider the following statement (s) that is/are correct about Communist Party.

 (i) It believes in radical and revolutionary socialism.
 (ii) It criticises Capitalism and Feudalism.
 (iii) It was against the policy of non-alignment and maintaining friendly relations with Soviet Union.
 (iv) They believe in the ideology of democratic socialism.

Codes

(a) Only (i)   (b) Both (i) and (ii)
(c) Only (iii)   (d) Only (iv)

Ans. (a) Communist Party believes in radical and revolutionary socialism. It was formed on 26th December, 1925 with a view to fight for national independence and future of socialism.

8. One of the guiding principles of the ideology of the Swatantra Party was ....

(a) Working class interest
(b) Economy free from state control
(c) Protection of princely states
(d) Autonomy of states within the union

Ans. (b) One of the guiding principles of the ideology of the Swatantra Party was economy free from state control.

9. Which among the following statements is wrong regarding First General Election?

(a) First general election was postponed three times in a row.
(b) It was held from October 1951 to February 1952.
(c) It was also known as 1952 Elections.
(d) All of the above

Ans. First general election was postponed twice and finally, it was held from October 1951 to February 1952. The elections were also referred as the 1952 election because most parts of the country voted in January 1952.

10. "The Congress Party was a social and ideological coalition." In the light of the statement consider the following statements.

(i) The Congress was a platform for numerous interest groups.

(ii) A coalition accommodates all those who are part of it and strike a balance on almost all issues.

(iii) The coalition nature of Congress failed to developed a greater tolerance of internal differences.

Which of the above statements are correct?

(a) (i) and (ii) (b) (ii) and (iii)
(c) Only (ii) (d) (i), (ii) and (iii)

Ans. (a) The coalition nature of Congress developed a greater tolerance of internal differences and accommodated the needs and aspirations of various groups and leaders.

11. Select the correct statements/s regarding One Party Dominance.

(i) One-party dominance is rooted in the absence of strong alternative political parties.

(ii) One-party dominance occurs because of weak public opinion.

(iii) One-party dominance is linked to the nation's colonial past.

(iv) One-party dominance reflects the absence of democratic ideals in a country.

Codes

(a) Both (i) and (ii) (b) Both (iii) and (iv)
(c) Both (i) and (iii) (d) Only (ii)

Ans. (c) One Party Dominance is rooted in the absence of strong alternative political parities and is linked to nation's colonial past. Hence, both (i) and (iii) are correct.

12. The part that won the second largest number of Lok Sabha seats in the first elections was the ....

(a) Praja Socialist Party
(b) Bharatiya Jana Sangh
(c) Communist Party of India
(d) Bharatiya Janta Party

Ans. (c) The party that won the second largest number of Lok Sabha seats in the first elections was the Communist Party of India.

13. Choose the wrong statement from the given options.

(a) The power structure of India after independence was dominated by the Congress Party.

(b) Congress was very well organised and had organisational presence across India.

(c) Indira Gandhi dominated the Syndicate group.

(d) Split in the Congress Party was evident during the 1969 Presidential elections.

Ans. (c) Indira Gandhi did not dominate the Syndicate group rather she dominated the Requisitionists group.

14. Which of these statements about the 1967 election is/are correct?

(i) Congress won the Lok Sabha elections, but lost the Assembly elections in many states.

(ii) Congress lost both Lok Sabha and Assembly elections.

(iii) Congress lost majority in the Lok Sabha, but formed a coalition government with the support of some other parties.

(iv) Congress retained power at the centre with an increased majority.

Codes

(a) Both (i) and (ii)
(b) Only (i)
(c) Both (iii) and (iv)
(d) Only (iv)

Ans. (b) Congress won the Lok Sabha election but lost the assembly elections in many states. The Lok Sabha election of 1967 was to take place after India had four Prime Ministers.

15. Arrange the following events in correct sequence.

(i) Second General Elections

(ii) VV Giri elected as the President of India

(iii) Fourth General Elections

(iv) Congress (R)-CPI alliance won more seats in general elections

Codes

(a) (i), (iii), (ii) and (iv)
(b) (iii), (ii), (iv) and (i)
(c) (ii), (iv), (i) and (iii)
(d) (iv), (iii), (i) and (ii)

Ans. (a) Second general election was held in 1957.

• Fourth general election was held in 1967.

• VV Giri elected as the President of India in 1969.

• Congress (R)-CPI alliance won more seats in general election in 1971.

16. Which of the following statements about the Grand Alliance of 1971 is correct? The Grand Alliance

(i) was formed by non-Communist, non-Congress parties.

(ii) had a clear political and ideological programme.

(iii) was formed by all non-Congress parties.

Codes

(a) Only (i)
(b) Both (i) and (ii)
(c) Only (iii)
(d) All of these

Ans. (a) The Grand Alliance of 1971 was formed by non-Communist, non-Congress Parties. They did form a party but did not have a coherent political programme and lost the elections.

17. Study the picture and answer the following questions.

Which of the following statement about the cartoon is true?

(a) The emergence of opposition parties and their policies.

(b) The establishment of a system of free and fair elections.

(c) The dual role of the Congress during the era of one-party dominance.

(d) None of the above

Ans. (c) The cartoon depicts the dual role of the Congress during the era of one party dominance. This was one of the famous cartoon sketched by Shankar.

• Assertion-Reasoning MCQs

Directions (Q. Nos. 18-20) In the following questions, a statement of Assertion (A) is followed by a statement of Reason (R).

Codes

(a) Both A and R are true and R is the correct explanation of A.

(b) Both A and R are true, but (R) is not the correct explanation of A.

(c) A is true, but R is false.

(d) A is false, but R is true.

18. Assertion (A) Our leaders were conscious of the critical role of politics in any democracy.

Reason (R) They.did not see politics as a problem; they saw it as a way of solving the problems.

Ans. (a) Both A and R are true and R is the correct explanation of A. The leaders of the newly independent India decided to take the more difficult path and were committed to the idea of democracy. Democratic politics was an answer to how society needs to govern and regulate itself. While competition and power are the two most visible things about politics, the purpose of political activity is and should be deciding and pursuing public interest. Our leaders decided to take this route of politics for India.

19. Assertion (A) The elections had to be postponed twice and finally held from October 1951 to February 1952.

Reason (R) But this election is referred to as the 1951 election since most parts of the country voted in January 1951.

Ans. (a) Both A and R are true and R is the correct explanation of A. The elections had to be postponed since the majority of the population was able to vote in January 1952. It took six months for the campaigning, polling and counting to be completed. Elections were competitive — there were on an average more than four candidates for each seat. Half of the eligible voters turned out to vote on the day of elections. When the results were declared these were accepted as fair even by the losers.

20. Assertion (A) The Indian National Congress was expected to lose this election.

Reason (R) The Congress party, as it was popularly known, had inherited the legacy of the national movement.

Ans. (a) Both A and R are true and R is the correct explanation of A. The results of the first general election did not surprise anyone. The Indian National Congress was expected to win this election. The Congress party, as it was popularly known, had inherited the legacy of the national movement. It was the only party then to have an organisation spread all over the country.

• Case Based MCQs

1. Read the following passage and answer the questions given below.

India is not the only country to have experienced the dominance of one party. If we look around the world, we find many other examples of one-party dominance. But there is a crucial difference between these and the Indian experience. In the rest of the cases the dominance of one party was ensured by compromising democracy. In some countries like China, Cuba and Syria the Constitution permits only a single party to rule the country.   [Delhi 2019]

(i) Which political party dominated the political scene of India after independence?

(a) Bhartiya Jana Sangh   (b) Indian National Congress

(c) Swatantra Party   (d) Communist Party of India

Ans. (b) Indian National Congress dominated the political scene of India after independence.

(iii) For how many years one-party dominance was there in the Independent India?

(a) 10 years   (b) 12 years

(c) 15 years   (d) 17 years

Ans. (c) For 15 years one-party dominance was there in the Independent India.

(iv) Which of the following are the drawbacks of a single party rule?

(a) It tries to establish anarchy and tyranny.

(b) It brings crises of the constitutional order.

(c) It encourages more opposition parties.

(d) Both (a) and (b)

Ans. (d) The drawbacks of a single party rule is as it establishes anarchy and tyranny and brings crises of the constitutional order.

(v) In India, One-party dominance of single party was the result of ....

(a) General elections that gave majority to the party

(b) Consensus of people

(c) Democratic set-up of India

(d) All of the above

Ans. (d) In India, one-party dominance of single party was the result of general elections that gave majority to the party, consensus of people and democratic set up of India.

PART 2
Subjective Questions

• Short Answer Type Questions

1. Describe any four features of the Congress Party.
[CBSE 2020]

Or Explain any four reasons for the dominance of the Congress Party in the first three general elections.

Ans. The main features of the Congress Party are

- The Congress Party inherited the legacy of the national movement. It was the only party to have an organisation spread all over the country.
- The Congress Party was supported by elites, educated business classes and middle classes people. It also got support from peasants for its socialist nature.
- The leadership of the Congress expanded beyond the upper caste and upper class professionals to agriculture based leaders with a rural orientation.
- The Congress was a 'platform' for numerous groups, interests and even political parties to take part in the national movement. Many organisations and parties with their own constitution and organisational structure were allowed to exist within the Congress.

2. Describe any four features of the ideology of the Bharatiya Jana Sangh. [CBSE 2020]

Ans. The Bharatiya Jana Sangha was formed in 1951. Its main features are

- The lineage of Bhartiya Jana Sangh can be traced back to the Rashtriya Swayamsevak Sangh (RSS) and the Hindu Mahasabha before independence.
- It was different from other parties in terms of ideology and programmes. It emphasised the idea of one country, one culture and one nation. It believed that the country could become modern, progressive and strong on the basis of Indian culture and traditions.
- The party called for a reunion of India and Pakistan in Akhand Bharat.

- The party was in forefront of the agitation to replace English with Hindi as the official language of India. It was opposed to the granting of concessions to religious and cultural minorities.

3. If Bharatiya Jana Sangh (BJS) or the Communist Party of India (CPI) had formed the government after the first election, in which respect would the policies of the government have been different? Specify three differences each for both the parties.

Ans. If BJS or the CPI had formed the government after first elections, the differences would have been as follows

Bharatiya Jana Sangh

- The Bharatiya Jana Sangh was in the fore-front of the agitation to replace English with Hindi as national language.
- It opposed granting of concessions to cultural and religious minorities.
- Party would have attempted to establish Hindu Rastra and have replaced secular polity of country.

Communist Party of India

- Party favoured abolition of zamindari system and stood for giving proper wages to forced labourers.
- It worked for making 'Right to Work' as a Fundamental Right.
- It advocated giving more power to states.

4. Describe any four features of the Communist Party of India. [CBSE 2020]

Ans. The four features of the Communist Party of India (CPI) are

(i) The Communist Party of India is inspired by the Bolshevik Revolution in Russia and advocated socialism as the solution to problems affecting the country.

(ii) Soon after Independence, the party thought that the transfer of power in 1947 was not true independence and encouraged violent uprising in Telangana.

(iii) The basic question that troubled the party was the nature of Indian Independence.

(iv) In 1951 the communist party abandoned the path of violent revolution and decided to participate in the approaching general elections.

5. Name any two founder leaders of the Swatantra Party. Describe any three economic policies of this party. [CBSE 2020]

Ans. The two founder leaders of the Swatantra Party were C Rajagopalachari and KK Munshi. Three economic policies of the party were

- The Swatantra Party wanted the government to be less involved in controlling the economy. It believed that prosperity could come only through individual freedom.

- It criticised the development strategy of state intervention in the economy, centralised planning, nationalisation and the public sector. It instead favoured expansion of a free private sector.
- The Swatantra Party was against land ceilings in agriculture and opposed cooperative farming and state trading.

6. Assess the economic situation of India before the general elections of 1967.

Ans. The economic situation of India before the general election of 1967 was worse. Failure of monsoon and drought led to serious food crises. The crises deepened due to the condition of the country which was still recovering from China war. The food crises triggered off price rise as demand for food was much more than its supply. This led to hoarding and black marketing of the essential food items.

There was massive inequalities in income and wealth. Due to this, large number of people were poor and not able to afford the basic necessities of life. This period was also marked by depletion of foreign exchange reserves, drop in industrial production and exports.

7. How did the dominance of Congress Party in the First three general elections help in establishing a democratic set-up in India?

Ans. Dominance of Congress Party in the first three general elections helped in establishing a democratic set-up in India in the following ways

- The coalition nature of the Congress Party tolerated and in fact encouraged various factions.
- It accommodated the revolutionary and pacifist, conservative and radical, extremist and moderate as well as right, left and all shades of the centre.

8. Differentiate between One-party and Bi-party system with examples.

Ans. The difference between One-party and Bi-party system is explained below

One-party system	Bi-party system
It refers to a political framework where one or single political party forms and runs the government.	It refers to a political framework where two major parties dominate voting at all levels of government.
In China all powers are vested with the Communist Party of China.	The United States is an example of a two-party system in which the majority of elected officials are either Democrats or Republicans.

9. What does defection stands for in Indian politics? Highlight any two demerits of this practice.

Or Assess the role played by 'defections' in the Indian politics.

Ans. Defection was a factor in 1967 elections. It played an important role in formation and collapsing of government. Defection displays the behaviour of an elected representative who leaves the party on whose symbol he/she won and joins another party.

Two demerits of this practice were

(i) It causes instability within party.

(ii) It promotes political opportunism among party legislators.

10. What main objective did Indira Gandhi want to achieve by launching a series of initiatives under the Ten Point Programme in 1967? [CBSE 2020]

Ans. Following are the objectives Indira Gandhi wants to achieve by launching a series of initiatives under the Ten Point Programme in 1967

- She wanted to achieve control of banks, nationalisation of General Insurance as well as ceiling on urban property and income.
- Ten point programme also emphasised on public distribution of food grains, land reforms and provision of house sites to the rural poor.

11. Describe any two advantages and two disadvantages of 'coalition' government in India. [Delhi 2009]

Ans. The advantages of coalition government in India are

(i) Coalition government provides an alternative to form government, whenever there is a case of hung Parliament.

(ii) It gives small and regional parties to have opportunities to representation in government.

The disadvantage of coalition government in India are

(i) It leads to instability in government, as different partners pull the government differently and government finds itself unable to take right decision at right time.

(ii) It reduces the credibility of office of PM/CM as their tenure depends at the pleasure of coalition partners. It produces weak government.

12. The phrase 'Aaya Ram Gaya Ram' signifies which concept? Explain its impact on the Indian political system. [Delhi 2009]

Ans. The expression 'Aaya Ram Gaya Ram' became popular in the political vocabulary in India to describe the practice of frequent floor-crossing by legislators. The phrase became the subject of numerous jokes and cartoons. Ultimately, the constitution was amended to prevent defections.

Its impacts on Indian political system were:

- It leads to instability within a political party.
- It promotes political opportunism in political system.
- It erodes the faith, and trust of common in political system.
- It causes instable government.

13. Examine the factors which helped VV Giri to become the President of India.   [Delhi 2008]

Ans. During 1969 presidential election, a series of events took place which helped Shri VV Giri to become the President of India. These were

- The factional rivalry between the syndicate and Indira Gandhi, the then PM became public in 1969.
- Despite Indira Gandhi's reservations, the Syndicate nominated her long time opponent and the then speaker of the Lok Sabha, N Sanjeeva Reddy, as the official Congress candidate for presidential elections. Smt. Indira Gandhi reacted by encouraging the then Vice-President, VV Giri to stand for presidential eletion as an independent candidate.

• Long Answer Type Questions

1. Analyse the reasons for the dominance of Congress Party in the first three general elections.   [Delhi 2014]

or Examine any three reasons for the dominance of Congress Party in the first three general elections in India.   [All India 2014]

or Highlight any three major reasons for the dominance of Congress Party in the first three general elections after independence. [Delhi 2019]

Ans. The Congress Party succeed in maintaining its dominance till 1967 due to following reasons

(i) The roots of this extraordinary success of the Congress Party go back to the legacy of the freedom struggle. Congress was seen as inheritor of the national movement.

   Many leaders who were in forefront of the struggle were now contesting elections as Congress candidates.

(ii) The Congress Party was supported by elites, educated business classes and middle classes people. It also got support from peasants because of its socialist nature.

(iii) It had many popular faces like Jawaharlal Nehru, C Rajagopalachari, Vallabhbhai Patel, etc. Moreover, Jawaharlal Nehru was charismatic and very popular leader.

(iv) Congress worked at upper level as well as at grassroot level. Congress was popularised due to the participation in civil disobedience movement.

(v) During period of Nehruji, Congress attained mass popularity, but the powerful narrow elite of congress confined to benefit from the low level of political consciousness of the electorate.

(vi) The traditional loyalities made Congress a one-party dominance.

2. Why were the general elections of 1967 called as the political earthquake for Congress? Examine any four reasons.

Ans. The general elections of 1967 called as the political earthquake for Congress party. The results of 1967 elections jolted the Congress at both the national and state level. Congress managed to get majority in the Lok Sabha but with its lowest tally of seats and share of votes since 1952. The reasons behind this were

(i) The Fourth General Election held in 1967 was the first election to be held without Jawaharlal Nehru.

(ii) Congress was dominant party before 1967, but scenario was likely to change after 1967's election. Several non-Congress parties joined together to bring Congress down. They realised that their disintegration kept Congress in power. So, they joined to form a big alliance called Samyukt Vidhayak Dal.

(iii) Congress still managed to win in Lok Sabha election, but with the poorest performance ever. Congress lost in many states and influential leaders of Congress lost their positions.

(iv) Many Congress leaders left the party in order to join the other party. Local politics gained momentum. Defection and coalition played an important role and new elements were in the scene of electoral politics.

3. Briefly explain the role of opposition parties in India.   [All India 2011]

or During the early years of independence, despite the fact that the opposition parties had a token representation, they played a crucial role in maintaining the democratic character of the system. How?   [All India 2008]

or List any four activities of the opposition during the parliaments of 1952 and 1957.

or Describe the role of opposition parties in the first phase of democratic politics in our country which was quite unique.   [All India 2019]

Ans. At the time of independence, there were many opposition parties and after independence it increased, but it gained only token representation in the Lok Sabha and also in State Assemblies. Yet their presence played a crucial role in maintaining the democratic character of the system.

The four activities of the opposition during the Parliament of 1952 and 1957 are as follows

(i) These opposition parties offered sustained and principled criticism of the policies and practices of the Congress Party. This phenomena indicated the check and balance of power of the Congress.

(ii) In 1957, in Kerala, Congress was defeated by CPI and made government, but after that Congress dismissed the Kerala Government under Article 356. It was criticised by the opposition leaders and said that it was the first instance of the misuse of constitutional emergence powers.

(iii) In 1950, BJS was able to secure 3 seats and in 1957, it secured 4 seats. The party played the role of opposition and started agitation to replace English with Hindi as the official language and also advocated for the development of nuclear weapons.

(iv) The opposition parties prevented the resentment with the system from turning anti-democratic. These parties also groomed the leaders (young citizens) who wanted to shape the India as developed and powerful state.

4. Examine the major changes that the country witnessed at the time of fourth general election in 1967. **[All India 2016]**

or Why was the year 1967 considered as landmark year in India's political and electoral history? Explain. **[All India 2010]**

or Examine the grave economic crisis prior to the fourth general elections of 1967. Assess the verdict of the electorate based on the election. **[Delhi 2010]**

or How did the fourth general elections (1967) in India change the dynamics of Indian politics? **[All India 2009]**

Ans. The fourth general election held in 1967 was the first election to be held without Nehru. Congress was dominant party before 1967, but scenario was likely to change after 1967's election. Several non-Congress parties joined together to bring Congress down.

They realised that their disintegration kept Congress in power. So, they joined to form a big alliance called Samyukt Vidhayak Dal. Congress still managed to win in Lok Sabha election, but with the poorest performance ever, Congress lost in many states. Influential leaders of Congress lost their position.

Many Congress leaders left the party in order to join the other party. Local politics gained momentum. In Tamil Nadu, a non-Congress party won on its own for the first time. 1967 elections showcased the new element which never came into light. Defection and coalition played an important role and new elements were in the scene of electoral politics. This situation could not have remained isolated from party politics in the country. The opposition parties got together and formed anti-Congress fronts in some states.

This strategy was given the name of non-Congressism by Ram Manohar Lohia. He argued that Congress rule was undemocratic and opposed the interests of ordinary people. Therefore, the non-Congress parties were necessary for reclaiming democracy for the people.

5. Discuss the major issues which led to the formal split of the Congress Party in 1969. **[NCERT]**

or Describe any three major events that led to the formal split in the Congress Party in 1969.

Ans. Three major events that led to the formal split in the Congress Party in 1969 were as follows

(i) The political tension inside the Congress over the unsettled question of relation between its ministerial and organisation wings became more pronounced. Indira Gandhi had acquired a certain control over the government but after the blow suffered by the Syndicate in 1967 elections, she had hardly any organisational base in the party. The veteran leader wanted that Indira should not interfere in party affairs.

(ii) After retirement of Kamaraj as party President at the end of 1967, the other members of party foiled Indira Gandhi's attempt to have her own men elected to succeed him. But Nijalingappa was elected and none of the Indira Gandhi's men were elected to the new working committee. She did not want to harm the unity of the party and the existence of her government by creating a conflict with the organisational wing, as the party enjoyed only a small majority in Lok Sabha.

(iii) Indira Gandhi adopted a radical ten-point programme which included social control of banks, nationalisation of 14 private banks and abolition of the privy purse or the special privileges given to former princes. The Congress divided into two factions, one was right and second was left. Left attacked on Morarji Desai as the representative of big business houses. The defeat of the Congress formalised the split in the party. The Congress President expelled the Prime Minister from the party. Indira Gandhi claimed that her group was the real Congress.

6. Assess any three challenges that the Congress Party had to face during the period from 1964 to 1971. **[All India 2014]**

or Describe any three important events that led to the split in the Congress Party in 1969.

Ans. The three challenges that the Congress Party had to face during the period from 1964 to 1971 were

(i) **Political Succession** After Nehru, some outsiders had doubts that Indian democracy will not survive, meanwhile party President K Kamaraj, suggested Lal Bahadur Shastri's name as the Prime Minister, thus he became the second Prime Minister of India.

An abrupt end of Shastri led to challenge of political succession. This time, there was intense competition between Morarji Desai and Indira Gandhi. Finally, Indira Gandhi became the Prime Minister. She set out to gain control over the party and to demonstrate her leadership skills.

(ii) **Emergence of Non-Congressism** Opposition parties realised that the division of their votes kept the Congress in power. So that they joined together to form anti-Congress fronts. This strategy was named as non-Congressism by Ram Manohar Lohia.

The result of 1967 elections jolted the Congress at both centre and state levels. Many elite leaders of Congress parties came together to form joint legislative parties (Samyukt Vidhayak Dal). In most of the states, Congress lost and coalition government was formed.

(iii) **Split in the Congress** Indira Gandhi had to face internal challenge that was Syndicate, a group of influential Congress leaders who were in control of the party's organisation. Gradually, she attempted to assert her position within the government and the party. She choose her trusted group of advisers from outside the party. Slowly and carefully she sidelined the Syndicate. Meanwhile, President of India Dr Zakir Hussain was dead, the post of President fell vacant. Despite of Mrs Gandhi reservations, the Syndicate nominated N Sanjeeva Reddy's name as President. But Indira Gandhi Supported VV Giri as an independent candidate. The election ultimately, resulted in the victory of VV Giri and the defeat of Sanjeeva Reddy, the official Congress candidate. The defeat of the official Congress candidate formalised the split in the party Congress (O) which was Syndicate supported party and Congress (R) which was Indira Gandhi party.

7. What does the term Syndicate mean in the context of the Congress party of the sixties? What role did the Syndicate play in the Congress party?

[NCERT, Delhi 2008]

or Analyse the issue India vs the Syndicate. What type of challenges did the issue pose before Indira Gandhi? **[All India 2017]**

Ans. Syndicate refers to a group of influential, powerful and leading leaders of Congress. They had real organisational power with them. They played crucial role in the establishment of Shastri and Indira Gandhi as Prime Minister. Indira Gandhi sought their support to become in power. It was expected that after installation, Indira Gandhi would follow their advice.

Their advise proved to be crucial in Indira's cabinet members selection and in the formation and implementation of policies. But situation changed and Indira's negligent behaviour towards Syndicate annoyed them. Polarisation between them increased, finally, leading to split.

Congress split into two parts, Syndicate lead Congress was named Congress (O) and Indira Gandhi led Congress was named Congress (R). But after split, Syndicate led Congress claimed that real organisational power vested in them. They were the think tank and real decision makers. In 1971 elections, it became clear that still Indira Gandhi possessed the real power and Congress prestige.

• Case Based Questions

1. Read the passage and answer the questions below.

Indira Gandhi changed the Congress into highly centralised and undemocratic party organisation, from the earlier federal, democratic and ideological formation that Nehru had led .... But this ....

could not have happened had not Indira Gandhi changed the entire nature of politics.

This new, populist politics turned political ideology....... into a mere electoral discourse, use of various slogans not meant to be translated into government policies .... During its great electoral victories in early 1970s, amidst the celebration, the Congress party as a political organisation died. **—Sudipta Kavlraj**

(i) What according to the author is the difference between the strategies of Nehru and Indira Gandhi?

(ii) Why does the author say that the Congress party 'died' in the seventies?

(iii) In what way, did the change in the Congress party affect other political parties also?

Ans. (i) According to author, main difference between the strategies of Nehru and Indira Gandhi is that Jawaharlal Nehru made the Congress into federal, democratic and ideological party, whereas Indira Gandhi changed it into highly centralised and undemocratic party.

(ii) According to author, Congress party died in the seventies because Indira Gandhi changed the nature of the Congress system. This new populist politics turned political ideology into a electoral politics only for the sake of victories. The use of slogans were meant to catch the attention of public, not to be translated into government policies.

(iii) The change in the Congress party also affected the other political parties. They formed alliance and coalition to defeat the Congress. They also adopted populist and welfare measures and slogans to counter the Congress and catch the public attention.

2. Read the passage and answer the questions below.

"Patel, the organisational man of the Congress, wanted to purge the Congress of other political groups and sought to make of it a cohesive and disciplined political party.

He .... sought to take the Congress away from its all-embracing character and turn it into a close-knit party of disciplined cadres. Being a 'realist' he looked more for discipline than for comprehension. While Gandhi took too romantic view of "carrying on the movement", Patel's idea of transforming the Congress into strictly political party with a single ideology and tight discipline showed an equal lack of understanding of the eclectic role that the Congress, as a government, was to be called upon to perform in the decades to follow." **—Rajni Kothari**

(i) Why does the author think that Congress should not have been a cohesive and disciplined party?

(ii) Give some examples of the eclectic role of the Congress Party in the early years.

(iii) Why does the author say that Gandhi's view about Congress' future was romantic?

Ans. (i) Author thinks that Congress should not have been a cohesive and disciplined party because it will take away the inclusive nature of Congress which accommodated the different view points, interest groups of society within itself. It will make the party a close-knit party of disciplined group.

(ii) In the early years, the Congress was called a social and ideological coalition representing the different and diverse sometime contradictory interest groups, caste group, religious and language groups.

It also acted as a platform for numerous groups, interests like peasants and industrialists and even political parties to participate in national movement. Thus, Congress was rainbow coalition having different social and ideological groups.

(iii) According to author, Gandhi's view about Congress future was romantic because Gandhi view Congress as movement representing the diverse caste, creed, and culture. While to be a political party and compete with other political parties Congress should have tight discipline and single ideology that Patel wanted Congress to have.

3. Observe the cartoon given below carefully and answer the questions that follow.

(i) What does the cartoon represent?

(ii) Who were the members of this committee?

(iii) Who have been shown sitting on the top?

Ans. (i) The cartoon represent the scenario of candidates seeking ticket for election from Election Committee of Congress which decide the candidates of the Congress for election.

(ii) The member of the Election Committee were Nehruji, Morarji Desai, Dr. BC Ray and Maulana Azad.

(iii) Morarji Desai, Nehru, Maulana Azad, DP Mishra, PD Tandon, Govind Ballabh Pant, Rafi Ahmed Kidwai, Dr. BC Roy, Kamraj Nadar and Jagjivan Ram were shown sitting on the top.

4. Observe the cartoon given below and answer the following questions. **[All India 2008]**

(i) To which year does the cartoon refer?

(ii) Name the person for whom this comment 'Aaya Ram Gaya Ram' was made.

(iii) What is defection?

Ans. (i) Given cartoon refers to the year of 1967 when defection become an important feature of Indian politics.

(ii) The comment 'Aya Ram Gaya Ram' was made to refer Gaya Lal, an MLA from Haryana, who changed his party thrice in a fortnight.

(iii) Defection means an elected representatives leaves the party on whose symbol he/she was cluted and jeins another party.

Chapter Test

Objective Type Questions

1. Which of the statement is/are correct about the expression 'Aya Ram Gaya Ram'?
   (a) The constant realignment and shifting of political loyalties.
   (b) Frequent shifting of alliance groups.
   (c) Frequent change in government.
   (d) None of the above

2. The concept of Alliance politics emerged after ....
   (a) 1952   (b) 1957
   (c) 1967   (d) 1971

3. .... is an example of Multi-party system.
   (a) USA   (b) China
   (c) India   (d) Mexico

4. Which party dominated the first three general elections?
   (a) Communist Party of India   (b) Indian National Congress
   (c) Bhartiya Jana Sangh   (d) Socialist Party

5. The first general elections in 1952 involved simultaneous elections to the Lok Sabha and
   (a) the President of India   (b) State Assemblies
   (c) Rajya Sabha   (d) the Prime Minister

6. Which of the following was/were the causes for the defeat of Congress in 1967 general elections?
   (a) Increased mobilisation of regional, ethnic and communal groups.
   (b) Increasing unity among non-Congress parties.
   (c) Internal differences within the Congress Party.
   (d) All of the above

Short Answer Type Questions

1. What were the problems faced during 1967 Elections?

2. Explain the role of Syndicate in Indira Gnadhi's Government.

3. Differentiate between One-party, Bi-party and Multi-party system.

4. Mentions important features of Bhartiya Jana Sangha's ideology.

5. What is mant by non-Congressiam?

Long Answer Type Questions

1. Write a note on Congress dominance in the first general elections.

2. What were the events that led to split in Congress?

3. Explain the Multi-party Coalition System in India.

4. What is meant by 'Privy Purse'? Why did Indira Gandhi insist on abolishing them in 1970?

Answers

1. *(b)*   **2.** *(c)*   **3.** *(c)*   **4.** *(b)*   **5.** *(b)*   **6.** *(d)*

CHAPTER 02

Democratic Resurgence

In this Chapter...

- National Emergency
- Movements Before the Emergency
- Declaration of Emergency
- Democratic Upsurges
- Famous Personalities and their Theories

The existence of democracy in India over the years has failed to solve the problem of illiteracy and democracy. A chain of events between 1973 and 1975 brought new challenges to India's democratic politics and the institutional balance sought by the Constitution.

Such developments led to the imposition of state emergency in June 1975-77 across the country. The period of emergency is considered one of the most controversial period of independent India's history.

National Emergency

Since 1967 significant changes took place in Indian politics. Indira Gandhi emerged as a successful leader with huge popularity among the people. Party competition during this period became bitter and polarised. This period also witnessed tensions in the relationship between the government and the judiciary. The Supreme Court found many initiatives of the government to be violative of the Constitution.

The Congress termed this stand of the court as against the principles of democracy and parliamentary supremacy. Congress also described court as a conservative institution which was becoming an obstacle in the implementation of programmes for pro-poor. The opposition felt that the politics had been personalised and government machinery was being used to implement Indira Gandhi's personal authority. The split in the Congress increased the division between Indira Gandhi and her opponents.

Economic Situation

The social and economic conditions in the country didn't improve much despite the Congress had won the elections of 1971 on the slogan of **garibi hatao**.

The following points highlight the economic condition in India in the post-emergency Congress rule

- The Bangladesh worsened the conditions of Indian economy. Almost eight million people crossed over the East Pakistan border in India.
- After the Bangladesh war, US Government stopped all aid to India. Oil Prices increased manifold which caused all round increase in prices of commodities during this period.
- Prices increased by 23 per cent and 30 per cent in 1973 and 1974 respectively. People had to suffer lots of hardship because of high level of inflation.
- Industrial growth was low and unemployment was very high particularly in the rural areas.
- The failure of monsoons in 1972-73 resulted in a rapid decline in agricultural productivity. Food grain production declined by 8 per cent.
- There was a general atmosphere of dissatisfaction with the prevailing economic conditions all over the country. In this

backdrop, non-Congress opposition parties were able to mobilise the popular protests effectively.

- The Marxist group also launched arms struggle to overthrow the capitalist order and established political system. Maoist or Naxalites group were particularly strong in West Bengal, where the State Government took strict measures to suppress them.

Movements Before the Emergency

The **students' protests** in Gujarat and Bihar states which were ruled by Congress had far reaching impact on the state as well as national politics.

Protests in Gujarat

In January 1974, students in Gujarat started a protest against rising prices of food grain, cooking oil and other essential commodities as well as against corruption. Major opposition parties joined the students' protest and thus, it became widespread protest resulting into the imposition of President's rule in Gujarat. The opposition parties demanded fresh elections.

Morarji Desai, a prominent leader of Congress (O) was the main rival of Indira Gandhi. He declared to go on an indefinite fast if fresh elections were not held in the state. Under intense pressure from opposition and political parties, assembly elections were held in Gujarat in June 1975 and Congress was defeated in this elections.

Protests in Bihar

In March 1974 in Bihar, students came together to protest against the rising prices, food shortage, unemployment and corruption. They invited **Jayaprakash Narayan** (JP), who had given up active politics and was involved in social work. They requested him to lead the students movement.

He accepted it on the condition that the movement will remain non-violent and will not confine itself to Bihar. Jayaprakash Narayan demanded the dismissal of Congress Government in Bihar. He called for **Total Revolution** in the social, economic and political spheres for establishing true democracy.

He wanted to spread the Bihar movement to other parts of the country. In 1975, Jayaprakash led a peoples' march towards the Parliament. Along side the agitation led by Jayaprakash Narayan, a nationwide strike by all employees of the Railways was led by the George Fernandes.

Jayaprakash Narayan was supported by the non-Congress opposition parties like the Bharatiya **Jana Sangh**, the **Congress** (O), the **Bhartiya Lok Dal**, **Socialist Party** and others.

Thus, both Gujarat and Bihar agitations were seen as **anti-Congress**. They were seen as a protest against the leadership of Indira Gandhi; rather than the State Governments.

Naxalite Movement

In 1967 a peasant uprising took place in the Naxalbari police station area of Darjeeling Hills district in West Bengal under the leadership of the local cadres of the **Communist Party of India** (Marxist). Beginning from the Naxalbari police station, the peasant movement spread to several states of India and came to be known as the Naxalite movement.

In 1969, one branch broke off from the CPI (M) and a new party, Communist Party (Marxist-Leninist) (CPI-ML) was formed under the leadership of **Charu Majumdar**. It argued that democracy in India was pretence and decided to adopt a strategy of protracted guerrilla warfare in order to lead to a revolution.

Methods Adopted by Naxalites

- The Naxalite Movement has used force to snatch land from the rich landowners and give it to the poor and the landless.
- Its supporters advocated the use of violent means to achieve their political goals.
- The Naxalite Movement split into various parties and organisations. Some of these parties, like the CPI-ML (Liberation) participated in open, democratic politics.
- Many districts in nine states (Odisha, Bihar, Jharkhand, Chhattisgarh, Andhra Pradesh West Bengal, Madhya Pradesh, Telangana and Maharashtra) are affected by Naxalite violence. Most of these are very backward areas inhabited by adivasis.

Reason of Naxalite Movement

- In these areas the sharecroppers, under-tenants and small cultivators were denied their basic rights with regard to security of tenure or their share in produce, payment of fair wages etc.
- Forced labour, expropriation of resources by outsiders and exploitation by money lenders were also common in these areas. These conditions lead to the growth of Naxalite Movement.

Conflict with Judiciary Before Emergency

The Indian Government had many differences with the judiciary. There was a long drawn conflict between Parliament and judiciary over each other's roles.

There were three issues which emerged

(i) The Supreme Court said that the Parliament could not abridge Fundamental Rights including Right to Property.

(ii) The court said that the Parliament could not amend in such a way that rights got curtailed.

(iii) The Parliament amended the Constitution on the ground that Fundamental Rights could be abridged for implementing Directive Principles. The Supreme Court rejected this proposition.

All three factors strained the relations between the government and the judiciary. Further tension was added between executive and judiciary by the two developments.

A vacancy of Chief Justice of India arose in 1973. As per practice, the senior most Judge of Supreme Court was appointed as the Chief Justice. But in 1973, AN Ray was appointed as the Chief Justice removing the seniority of three judges which generated a political controversy. **Political ideology** and **constitutional interpretation** got mixed up rapidly. People close to Prime Minister started questioning the need for a judiciary and the bureaucracy committed to the vision of executive and the legislature.

Declaration of Emergency

On 12th June, 1975 another issue was raised in which ruling of the Allahabad High Court declared Indira Gandhi's election invalid. This petition was filed by **Raj Narain**, a socialist challenging Indira Gandhi's election as invalid as she used government servants for her election campaign. The High Court declared her election as invalid so legally she was no more an MP and therefore, could not remain the PM unless once again elected as an MP within six months.

A political turmoil emerged after the Allahabad High Court decision. The opposition parties led by JP Narayan organised a massive demonstration in Ram Leela grounds on 25th June, 1975 for resignation of Indira Gandhi. JP announced a nationwide **Satyagraha** for her resignation and asked the army, the police and government employees not to obey illegal immoral orders.

Indira Gandhi's government responded to this crisis by declaring a state of Emergency. On 25th June, 1975, the government argued that there was a threat of internal disturbances and therefore, she imposed Emergency under Article 352 of the Constitution. During the National Emergency, Indian Constitution provided it special powers to the government. These were

- Once an Emergency is proclaimed, the **federal distribution of powers** remain practically suspended and all the powers get concentrated to the Union Government.

- Government also gets power to restrict all or any of the Fundamental Rights during the emergency.

Emergency is seen as an extraordinary condition in which democratic politics cannot function normally.

On the night of 25th June, 1975, the President Fakhruddin Ali Ahmed was recommended to impose Emergency by Indira Gandhi. He immediately issued proclamation which was implemented on next day.

Consequences of Imposing Emergency

- With imposition of Emergency, agitation and strikes were stopped and banned. Many opposition leaders and workers were put up in jail and the political atmosphere became quite but little tense as well.

- Government suspended the **freedom of Press**. Press Censorship was imposed on newspapers and they were asked to get prior approval for all content to be published. This is known as **press censorship**.

- Due to fear of social and communal disharmony, government banned **Rashtriya Swayamsevak Sangh** (RSS) and **Jamait-e-Islami**. Protests, strikes and public agitation were not allowed.

- Fundamental Rights and Right of Citizen to move to the court for restoring their Fundamental Rights had also been suspended under the Emergency.

- The government made extensive use of **preventive detention**. Under preventive detention, people were arrested and detained not because they have committed offence but on the apprehension that they may commit an offence. Moreover arrested persons were not informed about the reason of their arrest and also could not challenge their arrest through habeas corpus petitions.

- Many cases were brought by and on behalf of arrested individuals in the High Courts and Supreme Court, but the government contended that it was not even necessary to tell the arrested individuals the reasons and grounds for their arrest. Several High Courts have ruled that a writ of **habeas corpus**[1] filed by a person challenging his or her detention can be heard even after the proclamation of emergency.

- The Supreme Court's constitution bench over-ruled the High Courts in April 1976 and approved the government's plea. It meant that the government may take away a citizen's right to life and liberty during an emergency. This judgement closed the doors of judiciary for the citizens and is regarded as one of the most controversial judgements of the Supreme Court.

- Many journalists were arrested for writing against the emergency.

---

1. **Habeas Corpus**[1] It is a writ issued by the Supreme Court of India to defend the Fundamental Rights of the citizens. Through this writ, Supreme Court/Hight Court orders one person who has arrested person to bring the body of the latter before the court.

- Kannada writer Shivarama Karnath awarded with Padma Bhushan and Hindi writer Fanishwaranath Renu awarded with Padma Shri returned their awards in protest against the suspension of democracy.
- Many political workers went underground and organised protest against the government.
- Newspapers like Indian Express and Statesman protested against the censorship by resorting to leave blank spaces of censored news. Magazines like Seminar and Mainstream were closed down.
- An amendment was made in the background of ruling of Allahabad High Court that henceforth, nobody can challenge the elections of PM, President and Vice-President.
- The **42nd Amendment** was also passed during emergency which was considered as the most controversial amendment. It attempted to reduce the power of the Supreme Court and High Court to pronounce upon the constitutional validity of laws. It laid down the fundamental duties of Indian citizens to the nation. This amendment brought about the most widespread changes to the Constitution in its history and is also called a **mini-Constitution** or the **Constitution of Indira**.
- The government also passed certain amendments to the Constitution curbing powers of judiciary and President. It even extended tenure of the Parliament from 5 to 6 years.

Controversies Regarding Emergency

The most controversial episode in Indian politics was Emergency due to the following reasons

- **Internal distrubances** as mentioned by the Constitution became the reason for declaring Emergency. Emergency was never proclaimed on this ground prior to 1975.
- There were differing view points on the need to implement emergency.
- By using the powers of Constitution, the government practically suspended democratic functioning.
- Investigations by Shah Commission later found out that excesses were committed during emergency.

Views in Favour of Emergency

- In a democracy the government argued that, opposition parties must allow the elected ruling party to govern according to its policies.
- It felt that frequent recourse to agitations, protests and collective actions are not good for democracy.
- Congress contended that use of extra-parliamentary methods hindered development and lead to instability as all energy had to be spent on maintenance of law and order.
- In this regard, Indira Gandhi wrote to Shah Commission that Emergency was implemented as subversive forces tried to dislodge the government by using extra-constitutional methods.
- Some parties like CPI backed the Congress during emergency and said there was an international conspiracy against the unity of the India.

Views Against the Emergency

- Leaders like JP felt that since independence people had a right to protest. Movements of Bihar and Gujarat were peaceful. Those arrested were never tried for anti-national activities. There was no need to implement measures like emergency to curb such protest.
- Critics of emergency argued that India had history of such movements including freedom movement and also people had the right to protest against government in democracy.
- Even the Home Ministry which was monitoring the internal situation of the country did not express any concern about law and order situation in the country.
- Even if some agitations had overstepped their limits, there was no need to suspend the democratic functioning of the country.
- Critics also held that Indira Gandhi had misused constitutional provision for saving her personal power instead of saving the country.

Issues During the Emergency Period

It was said that government misused its emergency powers in the name of maintaining law and order, restoring efficiency and implementing pro-poor programmes. For this purpose, Indira Gandhi launched **twenty point programme** which included

- Land reforms
- Land redistribution
- Review of agricultural wages
- Workers' participation in management
- Eradication of bonded labour, etc.

During the early months of Emergency, urban middle classes were happy that frequent agitation came to an end and discipline was enforced on government employees. The poor and rural people also expected effective implementation of the welfare programmes. Thus, different sections of society had different expectations from the Emergency and had different viewpoints about it.

Critics of emergency felt that promises made to the poor were to divert the attention of people from the excesses that were taking place. The Shah Commission held that nearly one lakh eleven thousand people were arrested under the **preventive detention laws** during Emergency.

There were other allegations against those who didn't hold any official position. Like Sanjay Gandhi the younger son of PM was not holding any official position yet he gained control over the administration and allegedly interfered in the functioning of the government. His role in the **demolition** and **forced sterilisation** in Delhi became very controversial.

Apart from the arrests of political workers and the restrictions on the press, the emergency directly affected the lives of common people. Torture and custodial deaths occurred during the emergency.

Arbitrary relocation of poor people also took place and over enthusiasm about population control led to cases of compulsory sterilisation.

Lessons Learnt from the Emergency

The Emergency showed both the **weaknesses** and **strengths** of India's democracy. Many observers thought that India ceased to be democratic during the Emergency but normal democratic functioning resumed within a short span of time. The lessons learnt from Emergency are discussed below

- It was proved that no emergency can destroy the democratic spirit of India.
- It brought out the ambiguities related to emergency provisions in the Constitution. Internal emergency can now be proclaimed only on the grounds of **armed rebellion** and any such advice to President must be written from the Council of Ministers.
- It made everyone aware of the **importance of civil liberties**. Courts also took an active role in restoring and protecting civil liberties of people.
- The most valuable lesson we learnt from emergency is that governments which are perceived to be **anti-democratic** are severely punished by the voters.
- Lastly we learnt that governments which are unstable and quarrelsome are punished by voters.

Politics After Emergency

The experience of emergency was quite visible in 1977 Lok Sabha elections. The 1977 elections after emergency was decisive as opposition parties fought on the slogan of **save democracy**. All the leaders and activists were released from the jail. All the major opposition parties came together on the eve of elections and formed a new party known as **Janata Party** under the leadership of Jayaprakash Narayan.

Some leaders of the Congress who were opposed to the Emergency also became part of this new party. Some of the Congress leaders also came out and formed a separate party under the leadership of **Jagjivan Ram** named as Congress for democracy, but later it merged with Janata party. The Janata Party campaign focused on the non-democratic character of the rule and on the various excesses that took place during the Emergency period.

The formation of Janata Party also ensured that non-Congress votes would not be divided. The results took everyone by surprise as for the first time since Independence the Congress party got defeated in the Lok Sabha elections and was able to win only 154 seats and its shares of votes fell to less than 35%. The Janata Party and its allies won 330 seats out of 542 in the Lok Sabha and Janata party itself won 295 seats and thus enjoyed a clear majority.

The Congress lost in every constituency in Bihar, Delhi, Haryana and Punjab and could win only one seat in Rajasthan and Madhya Pradesh and retained many seats in Maharashtra, Gujarat and Orissa and virtually swept through the Southern States. Indira Gandhi was defeated from Rae Bareli as was her son Sanjay Gandhi from Amethi. The middle class from North India were beginning to move away from the Congress and the Janata Party became a platform for many of the sections to come together.

Democratic Upsurges

Increasing participation of the people in the democratic politics of the country is broadly characterised as democratic upsurge. Based on this principle, social scientists have characterised three democratic upsurges in post-independence history of India.

The **first democratic upsurge** could be attributed from the 1950s till 1970s which was based on the participation of Indian adult voters to the democratic politics both at the centre and in states. Falsifying the Western myth that the success of democracy requires modernisation, urbanisation, education and access to media, the successful holding of elections to both Lok Sabha and legislative assemblies all across states on the principle of parliamentary democracy were the testimony of India's first democratic upsurge.

During the 1980's, the increasing political participation of the lower classes of the society such as SCs, STs and OBCs has been interpreted as **second democratic upsurge** by Yogendra Yadav. This participation has made Indian politics more accommodative and accessible for these classes. Although this upsurge has not made any major change in the standard of living of these classes, especially Dalits, the participation of these classes into the organisational and political platforms gave them the opportunity to strengthen their self- respect and ensure empowerment in the democratic politics of the country.

The era of **Liberalisation**, **Privatisation** and **Globalisation** from the early 1990s is attributed to the emergence of a competitive market society encompassing all important sectors of economy, society and polity thus paving way for the **third democratic upsurge**. The third democratic upsurge represents a competitive electoral market which is based not on the principle of survival of the best but rather the survival of the ablest.

It underlines three shifts in India's electoral market: from State to Market, from Government to Governance, from State as Controller to State as Facilitator. Moreover, the third democratic upsurge seeks to promote the participation of the youth who constitute a significant part of Indian society and have emerged as the real game changers in view of their increasing electoral preference for both development and governance in India's contemporary democratic politics.

Famous Personalities and their Theories
Jayaprakash Narayan and Total Revolution

Jayaprakash Narayan, popularly referred to as **JP** or **Lok Nayak** (The People's Leader), was an Indian independence **activist**, **theorist**, **socialist** and **political leader**.

Jayaprakash Narayan is known for three key contributions

(i) Fight against Corruption.

(ii) Principle of Communitarian Socialism.

(iii) Championing of 'Total Revolution'.

He was the first leader in post-independence India who undertook a tirade against corruption through the participation of youth, particularly in Gujarat and Bihar. He advocated the office of Lokpal against corruption. His principle of **Communitarian Socialism** views India as a society of communities encompassing three key layers, viz., **community**, **region** and **rashtra**– all combined together as an example of true federation.

Based on the above principles, Jayaprakash Narayan advocated transformation of individual, society and state through his call for **Total Revolution**. His call for total revolution sought to encompass moral, cultural, economic, political, educational and ecological transformations.

His political transformation included the right to recall, the importance of village/mohalla samities in democratic politics and his call for 'Upper Ke Log' to join political struggle for a clean politics in the country. The essence for transformation according to Jayaprakash Narayan revolves around 'Man' who could be the real catalyst of change in India.

Concept of Total Revolution

He defined Total Revolution as a combination of seven revolutions

(i) Social Revolution (Establishing equality and brotherhood in the society).

(ii) Economic Revolution (Decentralisation of economy and making efforts to bring about economic equality by taking village as the unit of development).

(iii) Political Revolution (Ending political corruption, decentralisation of politics and making public partner by giving them more rights).

(iv) Cultural Revolution (Defending Indian culture and regeneration of cultural values in common man).

(v) Educational Revolution (Making education occupation based and changing of education system).

(v) Spiritual Revolution (Developing moral and spiritual values and turning materialism towards spirituality).

(vi) Thought Revolution (Revolution in the way of thinking).

(vii) Ideological or intellectual (To bring change in society in time with ideas of Sarvodaya).

Ram Manohar Lohia and Socialism

Ram Manohar Lohiya was a socialist leader and thinker, freedom fighter and among the founders of the Congress Socialist Party, after the split in the parent party, the leader of the Socialist Party and later Samyukta Socialist Party member. He was one of the proponents of socialism in India. He championed the idea of **Democratic Socialism** while associating with democracy. Lohia considered both **capitalism** and **communism** equally irrelevant for Indian society. His principle of Democratic Socialism has two objectives

(i) The economic objective in the form of food and housing.

(ii) The non-economic objective in the form of democracy and freedom.

Lohiya advocated **Chouburja Rajneeti** in which he opines four pillars of politics as well as socialism: **Centre**, **Region**, **District** and **Village** – all are linked with each other. Giving consideration to affirmative action, Lohiya argued that the policy of affirmative action should not only be for the downtrodden but also for the women and the non-religious minorities.

Based on the premise of Democratic Socialism and Chouburja Rajneeti, Lohiya supported a **Party of Socialism** as an attempt of merging all political parties. The Party of Socialism according to Lohiya should have three symbols, viz., Spade (prepared to make efforts), Vote (power of voting) and Prison (willingness to make sacrifices).

Deendayal Upadhyaya and Integral Humanism

Deendayal Upadhyaya was a philosopher, sociologist, economist and politician. He presented the philosophy which is known as 'Integral Humanism' which was intended to present an 'indigenous socio-economic model' in which human being remains at the centre of development.

The aim of Integral Humanism is to ensure dignified life for every human being while balancing the needs of the individual and society. It supports sustainable consumption of natural resources so that those resources can be replenished. Integral Humanism enhances not only political but also economic and social democracy and freedom.

As it seeks to promote diversity, it is best suited for a country as diverse as India. The Philosophy of Integral Humanism is based on the following three principles

(i) Primacy of whole   (ii) Supremacy of Dharma

(iii) Autonomy of Society

Pandit Deendayal Upadhyaya opposed both Western **capitalist individualism** and **Marxist socialism**. According to him, capitalist and socialist ideologies only consider the needs of the human body and mind, so they are based on materialistic purpose whereas spiritual development is equally considered important for the complete development of human being which is missing in both capitalism and socialism.

His philosophy was based on the internal conscience, pure human soul to be called **Chhitti**, Deendayal Upadhyaya envisaged a classless, casteless and conflict-free social system. He advocated Indianisation of Democracy, particularly with a focus on Economic Democracy.

For him, **Decentralisation** and **Swadeshi** are the foundation of economic democracy. His philosophy broadly revolved around the principle of **Arthayaam** which states that both the absence and prominence of arths lead to the destruction and denigration of **Dharma** which is central to Integral Humanism.

Chapter Practice

Objective Questions

• Multiple Choice Questions

1. Which judge of the Allahabad High Court declared Indira Gandhi's election as invalid?
(a) Om Prakash Trivedi
(b) Jagmohan Lal Sinha
(c) Narain Dutt Ojha
(d) Kunj Behari Srivastava

Ans. (b) Jagmohan Lal Sinha, the judge of Allahabad High Court declared Indira Gandhi's election as invalid.

2. Which of the following were included in the Twenty Point Programme launched by Indira Gandhi?
(a) Land redistribution
(b) Land reforms, review of agricultural wages
(c) Workers participation in management, eradication of bonded labour
(d) All of the above

Ans. (d) The Twenty Point Programme of Indira Gandhi included land reforms, land redistribution, review of agricultural wages, worker's participation in management, eradication of bonded labour etc.

3. Which of the following were the consequences of emergency imposed in 1975?
(a) The government made large scale arrest under preventive detention
(b) Press Censorship was imposed on newspapers
(c) Fundamental Right were suspended
(d) All of the above

Ans. (d) The consequences of emergency imposed in 1975 were that the government made large scale arrest under preventive detention, the press censorship was imposed on newspapers and the fundamental rights were suspended.

4. Name the leaders who founded the Communist Party of India (Marxist Leninist).
(a) Jayaprakash Narayan   (b) George Fernandes
(c) Charu Majumdar   (d) P Sundarayya

Ans. (c) Charu Majumdar founded the Communist Party of India (Marxist Leninist). It argued that democracy in India was a sham and decided to adopt a strategy of protracted guerrilla warfare in order to lead to a revolution.

5. Which of the following statement (s) is/are correct about the proclamation of emergency in 1975?
(a) Power politics became personalised
(b) Bitter party competition
(c) Tensed relations between the government and judiciary
(d) All of the above

Ans. (d) The proclamation of emergency in 1975 made party competition bitter, tensed the relations between the government and judiciary and the power politics became more personalised.

6. Consider the following statement(s) correct about the downfall of the Janata government.
(a) The Janata Party could not keep together due to the internal conflict
(b) It had good leaders
(c) It lacked common programme
(d) Both (a) and (c)

Ans. (d) The downfall of Janata government was because it could not keep together the party and its people due to the internal conflict and it lacked the common programme.

7. Arrange the following in correct chronology.
(i) Shah Commission Appointed
(ii) Railway Strike led by George Fernandes
(iii) Declaration of Emergency by President Fakhruddin All Ahmed
(iv) Peasant uprising in Naxalbari Police Station
Codes
(a) (i), (ii), (iii) and (iv)   (b) (iv), (ii), (iii) and (i)
(c) (ii), (i), (iv) and (iii)   (d) (iii), (i), (ii) and (iv)

Ans. (b) The correct chronology is
* Peasant uprising in Naxalbari Police Station– 1967
* Railway strike led by George Fernandes–1974
* Declaration of Emergency by President Fakhruddin Ali Ahmed–1975
* Shah Commission was appointed in–1977

8. Choose the wrong statement from the given options.
   (a) Lohiya was one of the proponents of socialism in India.
   (b) Deendayal Upadhayaya championed the idea of 'Democratic Socialism' while associating with democracy.
   (c) Lohiya was a leader of Socialist Party.
   (d) Lohia considered both capitalism and communism equally irrelevant for Indian society.

Ans. (b) Ram Manohar Lohia has championed the idea of Democratic Socialism while associating his socialism with democracy. He considered both capitalism and communism equally irrelevant for Indian society.

   Hence, statement (b) is incorrect.

9. Why did the Janata Party government appoint a Commission of Inquiry headed by Justice JC Shah in May 1977? **[CBSE 2020]**
   (a) To inquire into several aspects of allegations of abuse of authority, excesses and malpractices committed during Emergency.
   (b) To inquire into matters related to constitutional provisions.
   (c) To give suggestive measures to the government regarding the actions taken during Emergency.
   (d) All of the above

Ans. (a) Janata Party government appointed a Commission of Inquiry headed by Justice JC Shah in May 1977 to inquire into several aspects of allegations of abuse of authority, excesses and malpractices committed during emergency.

10. Consider the following statements regarding the Emergency and select the incorrect one.
   (a) It was declared in 1975 by Indira Gandhi.
   (b) It led to the suspension of all Fundamental Rights.
   (c) It was proclaimed due to the deteriorating economic conditions.
   (d) Many opposition leaders were arrested during the Emergency.

Ans. (d) Option (c) is the incorrect statement regarding the emergency.

11. Find the odd one out in the context of proclamation of Emergency.
   (a) The Call for Total Revolution
   (b) The Railway Strike of 1974
   (c) The Naxalite Movement
   (d) The Allahabad High Court verdict

Ans. (c) The Naxalite Movement used force to snatch land from rich landowners and give it poor and the landless. Hence, it stands out in context of proclamation of Emergency.

12. .... helped in establishing equality and brotherhood in the society.
   (a) Social Revolution   (b) Cultural Revolution
   (c) Spiritual Revolution   (d) Thought Revolution

Ans. (a) Social Revolution helped in establishing equality and brotherhood in the society. It is a fundamental change in a society that involves a shift in power in a society.

13. Chouburja Rajneeti was advocated by which of the following leaders?
   (a) Fakhruddin Ali   (b) Charu Majumdar
   (c) RM Lohiya   (d) Jagmohan Lal Sinha

Ans. (c) Chouburja Rajneeti was advocated by Ram-Manohar Lohiya. Giving consideration to affirmative action, Lohia argued that policy of affirmative action should not only be for the downtrodden but also for women and non-religious minorities.

14. Study the picture given below and answer the questions that follows.

   Identify the person behind Indira Gandhi in the picture.
   (a) DK Barooah
   (b) Morarji Desai
   (c) Fakhruddin Ali Ahmed
   (d) JC Shah

Ans. (a) This picture appeared few days before the declaration of emergency and captures the sense of impending political crisis. The man behind the chair is D. K. Barooah, the then Congress President.

15. Study the picture given below and answer question that follows.

What was the slogan of Janata Party to campaign in elections?

(a) Save Democracy   (b) Save India
(c) End the Dominance   (d) End the inequality

Ans. (a) Save Democracy was the slogan of Janata Party to campaign in elections. Loknayak Jayaprakash Narayan was the founder General Secretary of the Congress Socialist Party and the Socialist Party. He became the symbol of opposition to Emergency and was the moving force behind the formation of Janata Party.

• Assertion-Reasoning MCQs

Directions (Q. Nos. 16-20) In the questions given below, there are two statements marked as Assertion (A) and Reason (R). Read the Statements and choose the correct option.

(a) Both A and R are true and R is the correct explanation of A.
(b) Both A and R are true, but R is not the correct explanation of A
(c) A is true, but R is false.
(d) A is false, but R is true.

16. Assertion (A) Fundamental Rights of the citizens were suspended till the continuance of National Emergency.

Reason (R) Due to different viewpoints of people about the imposition of Emergency, it is the most debatable and controversial topic of Indian politics.

Ans. (b) Both A and R are true, but R is not the correct explanation of A. The government gets the power to curtail or restrict all or any fundamental rights during the emergency. The Emergency gave dictatorial powers to a democratically elected government. Hence, it arose different view points of people regarding the imposition of emergency.

17. Assertion (A) According to few of the political parties in India, the emergency was necessary to control the deteriorating condition of the country politics.

Reason (R) The Communist Party of India supported emergency due to international interference by using students as weapons for destroying democracy of the country, such bans on protest to some extent were necessary.

Ans. (a) Both A and R are true and R is the correct explanation of A. The CPI supported the emergency. According to CPI, there was a conspiracy to defame Indian democracy by using innocent students, making them protest and create a trouble to a democratic governance. Hence, some political parties felt the need of emergency to control the deteriorating conditions of the country.

18. Assertion (A) In the elections of 1971, Congress had given the slogan of 'Garibi Hatao' (remove poverty).

Reason (R) The social and economic condition in the country did not improve much after 1971-72.

Ans. (b) In 1971 election, the Congress gave the slogan 'Garibi Hatao' however, the social and economic condition in country did not improve. The Bangladesh crisis put a heavy strain on India's economy, after Pakistan war the US stopped all aid to India, oil prices increased etc. led to much hardship to the people. Hence, both statements are true, but R is not the correct explanation of A.

19. Assertion (A) Upadhyaya identified nationalism, democracy and socialism as three principal 'isms' that affected the west.

Reason (R) Among these three 'isms' nationalism was the oldest and the strongest.

Ans. (b) Both A and R are true, but R is not the correct explanation of A. Pandit Deendayal Upadhyaya was a philosopher, sociologist economist and politician. The philosophy presented by him is called Integral Humanism. He considered nationalism the oldest and strongest of all three 'isms'.

20. Assertion (A) The government suspended the Freedom of the Press and implemented press censorship during emergency.

Reason (R) Press used its freedom to provoke people to carry out unnecessary protests and demonstrations. Press was against the ruling government.

Ans. (c) A is true because deciding to use its special powers under emergency provisions, the government suspended the freedom of press. With freedom of speech being suspended as a Fundamental Right, the printing presses were raided and the circulation of newspaper were asked to take permission before publishing any piece.

• Case Based MCQs

1. Read the passage given below and answer the following questions.

Once an Emergency is proclaimed, the federal distribution of powers remains practically suspended and all the powers are concentrated in the hands of the Union Government. Secondly, the Government also gets the power to curtail or restrict all or any of the Fundamental Rights during the Emergency. It is clear that an Emergency is seen as an extraordinary condition in which normal democratic politics cannot function.

(i) Who among the following was the President of India during Emergency?

(a) V V Giri
(b) Morarji Desai
(c) Fakhruddin Ali Ahmed
(d) Ram Manohar Lohia

Ans. (c) Fakhruddin Ali Ahmed was the President of India during Emergency. He was the fifth President of India from 1947 to 1977.

(ii) On what grounds Emergency was imposed?
 (a) External threats   (b) Internal disturbances
 (c) Terrorist attacks   (d) Both (a) and (b)

Ans. (b) On the ground of internal disturbances, the Emergency was imposed. It was officially issued by the President under Article 352 of the Constitution.

(iii) Under which Article, Emergency was imposed in India?
 (a) Article 350   (b) Article 352
 (c) Article 356   (d) Article 360

Ans. (b) Under Article 352, the Emergency was imposed in India. The Emergency Provisions are contained in Part XVIII of the Constitution of India from Article 352 to 360.

(iv) Which of the following were the implications of Emergency?
 (a) All the powers got concentrated in the hands of the Union Government.
 (b) Government also get the power to curtail all or any of the Fundamental Rights.
 (c) Federal distribution of power remains practically suspended during that time.
 (d) All of the above

Ans. (d) The implications of emergency were
- All the powers are concentrated by the centre.
- Centre becomes entitled to give executive directions to a state.
- Government can curtail or all or any of the Fundamental Rights.
- The Parliament becomes empowered to make laws on any subject mentioned in State List.

(v) Emergency is an/a .... condition in which normal democratic politics cannot function.
 (a) helpful   (b) extraordinary
 (c) unnoticeable   (d) inconspicious

Ans. (b) Emergency is an extraordinary condition in which normal democratic politics cannot function.

Unnoticeable and inconspicious are opposite of extra ordinary.

PART 2
Subjective Questions

• Short Answer Type Questions

1. Why is the 'Emergency' and the period around it known as the Period of Constitutional Crisis? Explain.   **[Delhi 2013]**

Ans. The Emergency and the period around it can be described as a period of constitutional crisis because it had its origin in the constitutional battle over the jurisdiction of the Parliament and the judiciary. It was also a period of political crisis because the party in power had absolute majority and yet, its leadership decided to suspend the democratic process. The emergency is often regarded as a dark phase in independent India's history because this period was marked by controlled state incarceration, forceful prevention and government crackdown on civil liberties. There were reports of frequent human rights violations and the press being censored to a repressive extent.

The emergency was issued by President Fakhruddin Ali Ahmed under Article 352(1) of the Constitution and lasted 21 long months beginning 25th June, 1975 and going on until 21st March, 1977. Several other human rights violations were reported from the time, including a forced mass-sterillisation compaign headed by Sanjay Gandhi, the Prime Minister's son. The Emergency is one of the most controversial periods of independent India's history.

2. Explain the reasons for the students movement of 1974 in Bihar and role played by Jayaprakash Narayan in this movement.   **[Delhi 2014]**

Ans. Reasons for the students movement of 1974 in Bihar were as follows
- Rising prices of foodgrains, cooking oil and other essential commodities and corruption in high places.
- There was a demand for fresh elections to the State Legislature. Morarji Desai, a prominent leader of Congress (O), who was the main rival of Indira Gandhi, announced that he would go on an indefinite fast if fresh elections were not held in the state.

Role played by Jayaprakash Narayan in this movement was as follows
- He demanded the dismissal of the Congress Government in Bihar and gave a call for total revolution in the social, economic and political spheres.
- A series of bandhs, gehraos and strikes were organised in protest against the Bihar movement. The movement was beginning to influence national politics. Jayaprakash Narayan wanted to spread the Bihar movement to other parts of the country.
- In 1975, JP led a peoples March to the Parliament. This was one of the largest political rallies even held in capital.

3. Highlight any two constitutional issues between the Parliament and the judiciary during the 1970s.   **[All India 2019]**

Ans. Two constitutional issues between the Parliament and judiciary during the 1970s were
 (i) On the issue of Fundamental Right and right to property, the Supreme Court denied the amendment to Constitution. While on the issue of Fundamental Right giving effect to Directive Principles, Parliament amended the Constitution, but later Supreme Court rejected it.
 (ii) Court gave a decision that there are some basic features of the Constitution and the Parliament cannot amend these basic features. This created tension between Parliament and Judiciary.

4. Analyse the grave crisis that compelled the government to impose a state of Emergency in the country. **[CBSE 2019]**

Ans. The grave crisis that compelled the Government to impose a state of Emergency were

- The opposition political parties led by Jayaprakash Narayan pressed for Indira Gandhi's resignation and organised a massive demonstration in Delhi's Ramlila grounds on 25th June, 1975.

- Jayaprakash announced a nationwide Satyagraha for her resignation and asked the army, the police and government employees not to obey "illegal and immoral orders." This too threatened to bring the activities of the government to a stand still. The political condition of the country had turned against the Congress.

- In the response government declared a state of emergency. On 25th June, 1975, the government declared that there was a threat of internal disturbance and therefore, it invoked Article 352 of the Constitution. Under the provision of this article the government could declare a state of emergency on grounds of external threat or a threat of internal disturbance. The government decided that a grave crises had arisen which made the proclamation of a state of emergency.

5. What reasons did the Government give for declaring a National Emergency in 1975? **[NCERT]**

Ans. The massive frequent protest, agitation and disruption led by the opposition parties under the leadership of JP and tussle between Indian Government and Judiciary prompted government to declare state of Emergency on 25th June, 1975. Government justified the declaration of Emergency on the following reasons

- There was a threat of internal disturbances which caused serious crisis which made declarations of Emergency necessary.

- In democracy, opposition parties must allow the elected ruling party to govern according to its policies. Frequent agitation, protest and disruption derailed government and democracy as well.

- Extra-Parliamentary politics targeting Government leads to instability and divert the focus of administration of law and order from development to maintenance.

6. The Shah Commission was appointed in 1977 by the Janata Party Government. Why was it appointed and what were its findings? **[NCERT]**

or Explain the findings of Shah Commission constituted after the end of Emergency of 1975. **[Delhi 2009]**

Ans. In May 1977, the Janata Party Government appointed Shah Commission of inquiry headed by Justice JC Shah, retired Chief Justice of the Supreme Court of India. It was appointed to look into the misuse of authority by government and conduct of unethical practices like demolition of Jhuggis, forced sterilisation, etc. which were conducted in the wake of Emergency. The commission gathered various evidences and recorded witnesses to give testimonies.

The findings of Shah Commission were

- It found out that Preventive Detention was widely used by the government. Around one lakh eleven thousand arbitrary arrests were made by the government.

- Newspapers were asked to get permission before publishing of any matter. In Delhi, Lieutenant Governor ordered General Manager of Delhi Power Supply to cut off the power supply of news press till they establish censorship apparatus.

- Jhuggi Jhopri were forcefully relocated in the barren area of Delhi and people were forcefully sterilised.

7. How did Janata Party make the 1977 elections into a referendum on the Emergency imposed in 1975? Explain. **[Delhi 2016]**

Ans. Janata Party made the election of 1977 into a referendum on the Emergency imposed in 1975 in the following ways

- Janata Party's campaign focussed on the non-democratic character of the rule and on the various excesses that took place during this period.

- In the backdrop of arrests of thousands of persons and the censorship of the press, the public opinion was against the Congress.

- Jayaprakash Narayan who led the party became the popular symbol of restoration of democracy.

- The party ensured that non-Congress votes would not be divided.

8. Why Janata Party could not maintain its position? What happened to it? **[NCERT]**

Ans. The Janata Party could not maintain its position because it was made up of different parties with different views and ideologies. Even the agendas of these parties were different. The only common agenda shared by all parties were to overthrow Indira's Government which they achieved, but after that the differences began to come up.

Disagreement could not maintain the stability for a long time. It cost its position after a short span of time. In 1980, again elections were held and Janata Party lost its position to the Congress. Congress won with good number of seats in Lok Sabha.

9. What were the reasons which led to the mid-term elections in 1980? **[NCERT]**

Ans. Janata Party had many differences within itself. It lacked direction, leadership and a common programme. The Janata Party could not make any fundamental change to policies. Disagreements among members prevented it to do so.

The Janata Party split after 18 months of its formation. Gaining from the scenario, Chaudhary Charan Singh formed its government with the support of Congress, but Congress withdrew its support after a short period of four months.

Thus, due to these reasons in 1980, fresh Lok Sabha elections were conducted in which Janata Party suffered a defeat and Congress seemed to gain its position back. Congress won 353 out of 542 seats in Lok Sabha. Congress restored itself again in 1980 Lok Sabha elections.

10. Analyse any three lessons learnt from the Emergency of 1975.   **[Delhi 2015]**

Ans. The three lessons of Emergency were

(i) Though many observers who thought that India ceased to be democratic during the Emergency but it proved wrong and normal democratic functioning reduced within a short span of time and in this context it is said that it is extremely difficult to do away with democracy in India.

(ii) Secondly, it highlighted some ambiguities regarding the Emergency provision in the constitution that have been corrected. Now 'internal' Emergency can be proclaimed only on the grounds of 'armed rebellion' and advice to President to proclaim Emergency must be given in writing by the Council of Ministers.

(iii) Thirdly, Emergency made everyone realised the value of the civil liberties. The court too have become active after the Emergency in protecting the civil liberties of the individuals.

11. Write a short note on Jayaprakash Narayan.

Ans. Jayaprakash Narayan, popularly referred to as JP or Lok Nayak (The People's Leader), was an Indian independence activist, theorist, socialist and political leader. Jayaprakash Narayan is known for three key contributions: Fight Against Corruption, Principle of Communitarian Socialism and Championing of 'Total Revolution'.

He was the first leader in post-independence India who undertook a tirade against corruption through the participation of youth, particularly in Gujarat and Bihar. He advocated the office of Lokpal against corruption. His principle of Communitarian Socialism views India as a society of communities encompassing three key layers, viz., community, region and rashtra– all combine together as an example of true federation.

12. Discuss the views against the Emergency given by the critics.

Ans. Some of the views against the Emergency are discussed below

- Critics of emergency argued that India had history of such movements including freedom movement and also people had the right to protest against government in democracy.

- As Emergency was imposed to curb the law and order situation but on the other hand, the Home Ministry which was monitoring the internal situation of the country did not express any concern about law and order situation in the country.

- Even if some agitations like Bihar and Gujarat had overstepped their limits, there was no need to suspend the democratic functioning of the country.

- Critics also held that Indira Gandhi had misused constitutional provision for saving her personal power instead of saving the country.

● Long Answer Type Questions

1. Why is Emergency considered to be one of the most controversial episodes in Indian politics? Analyse any three reasons.   **[Delhi 2009]**

Ans. Emergency is one of the most controversial episodes in Indian politics. Most of promises by the government remained unfulfilled that were simply meant to divert attention from the excesses that were taking place. They question the use of Preventive Detention on such a large scale. Many prominent political leaders were arrested. In all, 676 opposition leaders were arrested.

Some of the reasons are discussed below

- The Shah Commission estimated that nearly one lakh eleven thousand people were arrested under Preventive Detention laws. Severe restrictions were put on the press, sometimes without proper legal sanctions.

- The Shah Commission report mentions that the General Manager of the Delhi Power Supply Corporation Received verbal orders from the office of the Lt. Governor of Delhi to cut electricity of all newspaper presses at 2:00 am on 26th June, 1975. Electricity was restored two to three days later after the censorship apparatus had been set-up.

- Democracy remained suspended during Emergency. Democratic way of expression of feeling, anger, dissatisfaction, etc through protest, agitation, etc were crushed bitterly by government. And Emergency was imposed by the Government despite having majority to crush the democratic movement against the ruling party.

- Government suspended the freedom of press, newspapers were asked to take permission before publishing any matter. Fundamental Rights of citizens were suspended including the right to move to the court for restoring Fundamental Rights.

2. Discuss the effects of Emergency on the following aspects for our polity.   **[NCERT]**

(i) Effects on civil liberties for citizens.

(ii) Impact on relationship between the Executive and Judiciary.

(iii) Functioning of Mass Media.

(iv) Working of Police and Bureaucracy.

Ans (i) **Effect on Civil Liberties for Citizens**

- Large scale arrest of leaders and workers of the opposition parties were made under Preventive Detention act.
- Forced relocation and sterilisation of poor.
- Suspension of Fundamental Rights and available constitutional remedies.

(ii) **Impact on Relationship between the Executive and Judiciary**

- Rising conflict between government and judiciary.
- In the background of the ruling of Allahabad High Court, an amendment was brought that elections of Prime Minister, President and Vice President cannot be challenged in the court.
- 42nd Amendment was also passed to bring series of changes in constitution like duration of legislature, etc.

(iii) **Functioning of Mass Media**

- Government imposed press censorship suspending the freedom of press, newspapers and magazine to publish anti-government contents. Newspapers were asked to get prior permission from government before publishing any content.
- Newspaper like Indian Express and Statesmen protested against press censorship by leaving blank spaces where news items were censored.

(iv) **Working of Police and Bureaucracy**

- Government used police and bureaucracy to commit suppression, torture and atrocities on leaders and workers of opposition parties.
- Police and bureaucracy were misused to meet agenda of ruling party.

3. Describe any three major political developments that took place in India after the lifting of Emergency in 1977.

Ans. Three major political developments that took place in India after the lifting of Emergency in 1977 were as follows

(i) **Janata Party** It accepted the leadership of Jayaprakash Narayan. Some leaders of the Congress who opposed the Emergency also joined this new party. Some other Congress leaders also came out and formed a separate party under the leadership of Jagjivan Ram. This party named as Congress for Democracy which later merged with the Janata Party. Janata Party made this election into a referendum on the Emergency. Its campaign was focussed on the non-democratic character of the rule and torture, atrocities, supression, etc that took place during Emergency.

(ii) **Result of 1977 Elections** The final result of 1977 election was surprising because the Congress was defeated in the Lok Sabha elections for the first time since independence. In North India, it was a massive electoral wave against the Congress. The Congress lost in every constituency in Bihar, Uttar Pradesh, Delhi, Haryana and the Punjab. It could hardly won any seat each in Rajasthan and Madhya Pradesh. Indira Gandhi was defeated from Rae Bareli and her son Sanjay Gandhi from Amethi. The impact of Emergency was not felt equally in all the states.

The forced relocations and displacements, the forced sterilisation, were mostly concentrated in the Northern states. The middle castes from North India were moving away from the Congress and Janata party became a platform for many of these sections to come together.

(iii) **Split between Janata Government and Janata Party** Janata Party Government that came to power after 1977 elections was far from unity. There was stiff competition among Morarji Desai, Charan Singh and Jagjivan Ram for the post of Prime Minister. Finally, Morarji Desai became the Prime Minister but internal power struggle within the party continued.

The Janata Party Government did not bring any fundamental change in policies that pursued by the Congress. The Janata Party split and the government led by Morarji Desai lost its majority in less than 18 months. Another Government headed by Charan Singh was formed on the assurance of the support of the Congress party.

Fresh elections to Lok Sabha were held in January 1980 in which Janata Party lost badly, particularly in North India where it had swept the polls in 1977. Congress party under the leadership of Indira Gandhi repeated its great victory. It won 353 seats and form the government.

4. Explain the major outcome of 1977 Lok Sabha elections.

Ans. The major outcomes of 1977 Lok Sabha elections were

- The Janata Party successfully achieved what it desired for. The democratic outlook attracted the masses and result of 1977 Lok Sabha elections worked in its favour.
- The result of 1997 Lok Sabha elections was a big shock and surprise to Congress and Janata Party respectively.
- It was for the first time when Congress had lost the election at centre ever since the independence.
- Janata Party won 330 out of 542 seats, while Congress had to satisfy with only 154 seats.
- In North India, Congress had bitterest experience. In Bihar, Uttar Pradesh, Delhi, Haryana and Punjab, Congress rule was outrightly rejected.
- Indira Gandhi from Rae Bareli and her son Sanjay Gandhi from Amethi were defeated too.
- Congress manages to save many seats in Maharashtra, Gujarat, Odisha and Southern states and this was a great relief to the Congress.

- Congress managed to do so, because the impact of Emergency was comparatively less in Southern part. North India witnessed the harshest measures like displacement of people, sterilisation, etc. Janata Party also gave a perfect alternative to the people of North India. People began to move away from Congress, specially the middle class.

5. Analyse the circumstances responsible for the declaration of a state of Emergency in India on 25th June, 1975. **[Delhi 2016]**

Ans. The circumstances which led to the proclamation of Emergency were

(i) Bihar and Gujarat's movement created an unrest in the country. Students were protesting against the price rise and against the established Government in the states. Congress as ruling party failed to handle these protests. Leadership by influential leaders further gave them a momentum against government.

(ii) Increase in Naxalite activities against government and violent nature troubled the government. Naxalite had an anti- government view. Even harsh measures by government could not stop them.

(iii) George Fernandes gave a call for nationwide strike to all the railwaymen. Their demands were suppressed by the government. Shutdown of such a big institution created a havoc in the country.

(iv) Declaration of Indira Gandhi's 1971 election invalid was a last straw. Jayaprakash Narayan organised a massive demonstration demanding her resignation. The situation was tense and Emergency was declared on 25th June, 1975.

(v) Call of total revolution by Jayaprakash Narayan and unexpected people movement in Delhi.

(vi) Jayaprakash Narayan announced a nationwide Satyagraha for resignation and asked the army, the police and government employees not to obey illegal and immoral orders.

6. Evaluate the consequences of declaration of Emergency in 1975. **[All India 2014]**

Ans. Consequences of declaration of Emergency in 1975 were as follows

(i) During Emergency, democracy was suspended the federal distribution of powers remains practically suspended and all the powers were concentrated in the hands of the Union Government. It was made clear that a democratic country like India could not do away from democracy. Wide protest against Emergency arose to restore democracy.

(ii) Several changes to Constitution came into existence, e.g. election of Prime Minister, President and Vice President could not be challenged in the Supreme Court. 42nd Amendment came during this time and duration of legislature increased from 5 to 6 years.

(iii) The government also gets the power to curtail or restrict all or any of the Fundamental Rights during the Emergency.

(iv) During Emergency, government gets extra powers. They have the power to suspend the Fundamental Rights of the citizens. Measures like Preventive Detention could be used by government. Right to move the court for the restoration of Fundamental Rights were taken away.

(v) Government ordered newspaper press to censor the matter. The prior approval of government was made necessary before publishing any article in newspaper to avoid anti-government feeling.

7. Explain the three democratic upsurges that emerged in the post- independence history of India.

Ans. Increasing participation of the people in the democratic politics of the country is broadly characterised as democratic upsurge. Social scientists have characterised three democratic upsurges in post-independence history of India that are discussed below

- The 'First Democratic Upsurge' could be attributed from the 1950s till 1970s which was based on the participation of Indian adult voters to the democratic politics both at the centre and in states. Falsifying the western myth that the success of democracy requires modernisation, urbanisation, education and access to media, the successful holding of elections to both Lok Sabha and legislative assemblies all across states on the principle of parliamentary democracy were the testimony of India's first democratic upsurge.

- During the 1980's, the increasing political participation of the lower classes of the society such as SCs, STs and OBCs has been interpreted as 'Second Democratic Upsurge' by Yogendra Yadav. This participation has made Indian politics more accommodative and accessible for these classes. Although this upsurge has not made any major change in the standard of living of these classes, especially Dalits, the participation of these classes into the organisational and political platforms gave them the opportunity to strengthen their self- respect and ensure empowerment in the democratic politics of the country.

- The era of Liberalisation, Privatisation and Globalisation from the early 1990s is attributed to the emergence of a competitive market society encompassing all important sectors of economy, society and polity thus paving way for the 'Third Democratic Upsurge'. The Third Democratic Upsurge represents a competitive electoral market which is based not on the principle of survival of the best but rather the survival of the ablest. It underlines three shifts in India's electoral market: from State to Market, from Government to Governance, from State as Controller to State as Facilitator.

8. Explain the idea of Socialism advocated by Ram Manohar Lohiya.

Ans. Ram Manohar Lohiya was a socialist leader and thinker, freedom fighter and among the founders of the Congress Socialist Party, after the split in the parent party, the leader of the Socialist Party and later Samyukta Socialist Party member.

- He was one of the proponents of socialism in India. He championed the idea of 'Democratic Socialism' while associating with democracy.

- Lohia considered both capitalism and communism equally irrelevant for Indian society. His principle of Democratic Socialism has two objectives.

  (i) The economic objective in the form of food and housing.

  (ii) The non-economic objective in the form of democracy and freedom.

- Lohiya advocated Chouburja Rajneeti in which he opines four pillars of politics as well as socialism: Centre, Region, District and Village, all are linked with each other. By giving consideration to affirmative action, he argued that the policy of affirmative action should not only be for the downtrodden but also for the women and non-religious minorities.

- He supported a 'Party of Socialism' as an attempt of merging all political parties based on the premise of democratic socialism and Chouburja Rajneeti. The party of Socialism according to Lohiya should have three symbols, viz, Spade (prepared to make efforts), Vote (power of voting) and Prison (willingness to make sacrifices).

• Case Based Questions

1 Read the passage and answer the questions below.

Indian democracy was never so close to a two-party system as it was during the 1977 elections. However, the next few years saw a complete change.

Soon after its defeat, the Indian National Congress split into two groups ....The Janata Party also went through major conclusions............ David Butler, Ashok Lahiri and Prannoy Roy.

—**Partha Chatterjee**

(i) What made the party system in India look like a two-party system in 1977?

(ii) Many more two parties existed in 1977. Why are the authors describing this period as close to a two-party system?

(iii) What caused splits in Congress and the Janata Parties?

Ans. (i) The emergence of Janata Party as a majority winner at centre first time since independence looked like a two-party system.

(ii) Although more than just two parties existed in 1977, however, author described this period as close to a two-party system because only two major parties Congress and Janata Party have mass base support and mobilisation to form majority government.

(iii) The split in Congress took over the issue of Presidential election in 1969 and in Janata Party, split occured due to internal deadlock over the post of Prime Ministership in 1979.

2. Read the given passage carefully and answer the questions that follow.

The opposition to Emergency could keep the Janata party together only for a while. Its critics felt that Janata Party lacked direction, leadership and a common programme. The Janata Party Government could not bring about a fundamental change in policies from those pursued by the Congress. The Janata Party split and the government which was led by Morarji Desai lost its majority in less than 18 months. Another government headed by Charan Singh was formed on assurance of the support of the Congress Party. **[CBSE 2020]**

(i) In which year did the Janata Party government came to power?

(iii) Why could the Charan Singh government remain in power for just about four months only?

(ii) Which of the following reasons were responsible for the split of the Janata Party?

Ans. (i) Janata Party Government came to power in 1977.

(ii) Charan Singh government remained in power for just about four months only because it formed government on the appearance of the support given by the Congress Party and the party later decided to withdraw its support from his government.

(iii) The reasons responsible for split of the Janata Party were

- It lacked directions, leadership and a common programme.

- A stiff competition among the leaders of Janata Party for post of PM.

- There was no fundamental change in policies.

3. Observe the picture given below carefully and answer the following questions.

  (i) Identify and name the person holding in his hand, the placard 'save democracy'. In your opinion, the group of five persons belongs to which political party?

 (ii) According to the group of five, what are the intentions of the person sitting on 'Dharna'?

(iii) Which issues are responsible for the downfall of democracy are highlighted in the picture?

Ans. (i) Jayaprakash Narayan is holding the placard 'save democracy'. In the above picture, the group of five persons belong to Congress Party.

  (ii) The intentions of the person sitting on 'Dharna' are to support democracy, create chaos and grab power.

(iii) Corruption, lawlessness, violence, etc are responsible for the downfall of democracy.

4. Study the picture given below and answer the questions that follow.

  (i) What situation does the picture refer to?

 (ii) Which Commission is represented into the picture?

(iii) Mention some points of this Commission's report.

Ans. (i) Appearance of Indra Gandhi before Commission but refused to answer any question.

 (ii) Shah Commission is represented in the picture.

(iii) ▪ There were many excess committed during emergency.

    ▪ Several restrictions were put on the press sometimes without legal sanction.

    ▪ Many people were arrested under preventive detention law.

    ▪ Even general manager of Delhi Power Supply Corporation received verbal orders from the officers of Lt. Governor of Delhi to cut electricity to all newspaper presses at 2 am on 26th June, 1975.

Chapter Test

Objective Type Questions

1. Which of the following problems country faces during 1967 elections?
 (a) Period characterised by Serious economic crisis.
 (b) Depletion of foreign exchange reserves.
 (c) The devaluation of India Rupee.
 (d) All of the above

2. The demand for dismissal of Congress Government was demanded in Bihar because ....
 (a) To change the scenario
 (b) To establish true democracy
 (c) To conduct re-elections
 (d) All of these

3. In which year AN Ray was appointed as the Chief Justice removing the seniority of three judges which generated a political controversy?
 (a) 1971
 (b) 1972
 (c) 1973
 (d) 1974

4. In 1977 elections Congress party won only .... seats.
 (a) 120
 (b) 154
 (c) 155
 (d) 157

5. According to Deendayal Upadhayaya Swadeshi and .... are the foundations of Economic Democracy.
 (a) Development
 (b) Centralisation
 (c) Decentralisation
 (d) Inflation

Short Answer Type Questions

1. State any two reasons which added to Indira's problems after 1971 elections.

2. What was the reason behind the invalidity of Indira's 1971 election?

3. Explain Preventive Detention. How was it used during Emergency.

4. What was the explanation of government behind using draconian provisions of Emergency?

Long Answer Type Questions

1. On what grounds Emergency was declared on 25th June, 1975?

2. Explain the contest between Janata Party and Congress in 1977 Lok Sabha elections.

3. What special powers does a government enjoy during Emergency? How did it help Indira in 1975?

4. Highlight constitutional issues between the Parliament and the Judiciary during the 1970s.

Answers

1. *(d)* **2.** *(b)* **3.** *(c)* **4.** *(b)* **5.** *(c)*

CHAPTER 03

Indian Politics : Trends and Developments

In this Chapter...

- Development in Indian Politics
- Era of Coalitions
- Political Rise of Other Backward Classes
- Emergence of New Consensus
- Issues of Development and Governance

Development in Indian Politics
(Context of 1990's)

The trends and developments in Indian politics are complex at different stages. The advent of coalition politics has induced pronounced political changes but coalition politics itself can be seen as a consequence of these changes.

After the assassination of Indira Gandhi in 1984, **Rajiv Gandhi** became the Prime Minister through a massive victory in the 1984 Lok Sabha elections. Some of the developments visible during the end of 1980's which made long-lasting impact on Indian politics are discussed below

End of Congress System

This period witnessed the defeat of the Congress party in the elections of 1989. The party that had won 415 seats in the Lok Sabha in 1984 was reduced to only 197 in this election. The elections of 1989 marked the end of the 'Congress System'. The Congress improved its performance and came back to power after the mid-term elections of 1991. The politics of this decade has clearly seen the impact of social change on political and electoral processes.

Mandal Issue

Second development was the rise of Mandal issue in the national politics. The new National Front Government in 1990 implemented the recommendation of the Mandal Commission. It held that jobs in Central Government should be the reserved for the OBC's. This caused violent anti-Mandal protests in different parts of the country.

The dispute was evident among the supporters and opponents of OBC's reservations came to be known as Mandal Issue. This issue helped in shaping Indian politics since 1989.

New Economic Reforms

It was initiated by Rajiv Gandhi in 1991 which changed the direction of the Indian economy that was pursued since independence. The new economic reforms were widely criticised by various movements and organisations. But various governments that came to power continued these policies. Reforms were evident in the form of additional sectors that were reserved for public investment was opened for private investment.

Ayodhya Dispute

Another issue was the demolition of Babri Masjid and rise of **Hindutva politics**. A number of events resulted in the demolition of disputed structure known as **Babri Masjid** in December 1992. This event brought various changes in the politics of the country and intensified debates on the nature of Indian nationalism and secularism. These developments led to the rise of BJP and politics of Hindutva.

Change in Congress Leadership

The last development was the assassination of Rajiv Gandhi in May 1991 led to change in the leadership of the Congress party. He was assassinated during his election campaign tour in Tamil Nadu by a Sri Lankan Tamil associated to the LTTE (The Liberation Tigers of Tamil Eelam). The Congress emerged as the single largest party in the elections of 1991 and Narsimha Rao was chosen as Prime Minister after the death of Rajiv Gandhi.

Era of Coalitions

With 1989 elections, an era of coalitions came up with the beginning of third electoral system. This era is built around the core principles that include a sharp rise in political competition at the national level and declining margins of victory in parliamentary races. With the defeat of Congress Party in the 1989 elections, no other party emerged in majority at the Central level.

Congress was the largest party in the Lok Sabha but as it didn't got clear majority so it decided to sit in the opposition. The National Front (an alliance of Janta Dal and other regional parties) got support from BJP and the Left Front. On this basis, the National Front formed the government but BJP and Left Front did not join this government.

Decline of Congress

The end of Congress dominance in the Indian party system emerged after the defeat of Congress in the elections. During the late 1960's, when the dominance of the Congress Party was challenged, Indira Gandhi successfully re-established its dominant position in politics. The era of 1990's witnessed another challenge to the predominant position of Congress as no single party could replace Congress.

This led to the emergence of multi-party system in the Indian political scenario. Since 1989 no single party secured a clear majority in any Lok Sabha elections. Thus, this development initiated an era of coalition government at the centre in which regional parties played an important role in forming ruling alliances. The vote share belonging to regional parties has expanded, while growth in voter turnout in national elections has halted and electoral politics has become 'federalised.'

National Front and United Front

Political alliance is an agreement for cooperation between different political parties on common political agenda, often for purposes of contesting an election to mutually benefit by collectively clearing election thresholds. The 90's witnessed the emergence of powerful parties and movements that represented the Dalit and backward castes (OBC's). These parties played an important role in the formation of United Front Government in 1996 which was supported by Congress.

Between 1989 and 1990, the National Front was a coalition of political parties led by the Janata Dal that constituted India's Government under the leadership of NT Rama Rao as President. Following the 1996 general elections in India, the United Front was created as a coalition government of 13 political parties.

Both Left Front and BJP supported the National Front Government as they wanted to keep the Congress out of power. Although in 1996, the Left Front continued to support the non-Congress government with Congress support to keep BJP out of power.

They didn't succeed for long because the BJP constantly consolidated its position of 1991 and 1996. BJP emerged as the largest party in 1996 elections as it was invited to form the government. Its policies were opposed by other parties so BJP could not secure majority in the Lok Sabha.

A coalition government was formed by BJP from May 1998 to June 1999 and it was re-elected in October 1999. During both these terms, NDA (National Democratic Alliance) i.e. BJP-led coalitions formed the government led by Atal Bihari Vajpayee as the Prime Minister.

A long phase of coalition politics began with the elections of 1989. Since then, there have been nine governments at the centre. All of which have been either coalition governments or minority governments supported by other parties. In this phase, any government could be formed only with the participation of regional parties. This was visible during for instance

- The National Front Government in 1989.
- The United Front Government in 1996 and 1997.
- National Democratic Alliance (NDA), BJP-led coalitions in 1997, 1998 and 1999.
- United Progressive Alliance (UPA) in 2004 and 2009.

However, this trend of coalition government changed in 2014.

Political Rise of Other Backward Classes

One long term development of this period emerged in the form of rise of Other Backward Classes (OBC's). Here, the term OBC refers to the administrative category OBC. These communities other than SC and ST who suffer from educational and social backwardness also referred to as backward castes. Many Non-Congress parties like the Janata Party government in 1977 supported these communities. Parties like Bhartiya Kranti Dal and the Samyukta Socialist Party also had a powerful rural base among sections of OBC.

Mandal Commission

Southern States have had reservations for the OBC since the 1960's, if not before.

However, this policy did not apply to the states of North India. The demand for reservations for backward castes in North India and at the national level was forcefully promoted during the duration of the Janata Party government in 1977-1979.

Following this, in 1978, the Central Government established a commission to investigate and recommend methods to ameliorate (improve) the conditions of the poor.

As a result, the commission was dubbed (termed) as the second backward classes commission. The Committee is commonly refered to as the Mandal Commission, after its chairperson, Bindeshwari Prasad Mandal.

- The Mandal Commission was set up to investigate the extent of educational and social backwardness among various sections of Indian society. It recommended ways of identifying these **backward classes**. It was also expected to give its recommendations on the ways in which this backwardness could be ended. The Commission gave its recommendations in 1980.
- The Commission advised that 'backward classes' should be understood to mean 'backward castes', since many castes, other than the Scheduled Castes, were also treated as low in the caste hierarchy.
- It recommended reserving 27 per cent of seats in the educational institutions and government jobs for these groups. The Mandal Commission also made many other recommendations like land reforms, to improve the conditions of OBC's.
- In August 1990, the National Front Government decided to implement one of the recommendations of Mandal Commission. It was related to reservations for OBC's in jobs at the Central Government level and its undertakings.

Consequences of Implementing Mandal Commission

- This decision caused agitations and violent protests in many cities of North India.
- The decision was also challenged in the Supreme Court and came to be known as the Indira Sawhney Case, after the name of the petitioners.
- In November 1992, the Supreme Court gave a ruling upholding the decision of the government.

Emergence of New Consensus

Sometimes the period after 1989 is seen as a period of decline of Congress and rise of BJP. Despite severe competition and many conflicts, a broad consensus emerged on many crucial issues. These were

- First agreement was on new economic policies. Most political parties have consensus about the new economic policies despite the fact many groups opposed this. As it was believed that these policies will bring prosperity and help the country to be an economic power in the world.
- Second was the acceptance of political and social claims of the backward castes. Most of the political parties accepted and supported the reservation of seats for the backward classes in education and employment. Political parties also ensure that the OBC's get adequate share of power.

- The third acceptance was the role of regional parties. The role of state level parties in governance of the country is accepted by all major parties. Regional parties are sharing power at the national level and has been playing central role in the politics of the country for twenty years.

- The fourth emphasis was on pragmatic considerations rather than the ideological. Most of the political parties' emphasis on practical considerations rather than ideological positions. The coalition politics has shifted the focus of political parties from ideological differences to power sharing arrangements. For instance, most parties of NDA didn't agree with the Hindutva ideology of BJP but they came together to form government.

Lok Sabha Elections, 2004

In the elections of 2004, NDA was defeated and new coalition government led by the Congress **United Progressive Alliance** came to power. This government also received support from the Left Front parties. The Congress also witnessed partial revival of Congress party. Its seats increased for the first time since 1991. But in 2004 elections, there was negligible difference between the votes polled by the Congress and its allies and BJP and its allies.

After 1990s, the political processes show the emergence of broadly four groups of parties

  (i) Parties which were in coalition with the Congress.

  (ii) Parties which are in alliance with the BJP.

 (iii) Left Front parties.

  (iv) Parties which are not a part of any of these three.

Thus, the party system has now changed from what it was till 1970s. And political competition was expected to be multi-cornered.

United Progressive Alliance (UPA) I and II

In the General Election of 2009, UPA won 262 seats, of which the Congress accounted for 206 seats. Manmohan Singh formed another UPA coalition cabinet and was sworn in for a second term, becoming the first Prime Minister since Jawaharlal Nehru to do so after having served a full five-year first term. The government made employment generation and social equity as the important features of its agenda.

Under UPA-II, women began occupying senior positions in State and Union Territory governments, notably in highly populated Tamil Nadu, Uttar Pradesh and West Bengal. It also works upon the issues of revitalising the agrarian economy, stepping up investment in agriculture, providing access to credit and improving the quality of rural infrastructure.

National Democratic Alliance (NDA) III and IV

The Bharatiya Janata Party led by Prime Minister Narendra Modi got an absolute majority in the Lok Sabha elections held in May 2014 and after nearly 30 years in Indian politics; a strong government with an absolute majority was established at the Centre.

Though called NDA III, the BJP-led coalition of 2014 was largely different its predecessor coalition governments. Where the previous coalitions were led by one of the national parties, the NDA III coalition was not only steered by a national party, i.e., BJP it was also dominated by BJP with an absolute majority of its own in Lok Sabha.

It was also called a **surplus majority coalition**. In that sense a major transformation could be seen in the nature of coalition politics which could be seen from one party led coalition to one party dominated coalition. The 2019 Lok Sabha elections, the 17th since independence, once again brought back BJP led NDA (NDA IV) to the centre of power by winning more than 350 seats out of 543.

The BJP on its own won 303 seats in Lok Sabha, the biggest number any single party has won in the lower house since 1984 when Congress swept the elections in the aftermath of Mrs Indira Gandhi's assassination. Based on the tumultuous success of the BJP in 2019, Social Scientists have started equating the contemporary party system with the 'BJP System' where an era of one party dominance, like the 'Congress System' has once again started appearing on the democratic politics of India.

Issues of Development and Governance

A major change in Indian politics after 2014 is the shift from caste and religion based politics to development and governance oriented politics. With its pre-intended goal **Sabka Saath, Sabka Vikas**, the NDA III Government started several socio-economic welfare schemes to make development and governance accessible to the masses such as

- Pradhan Mantri Ujjwala Yojana
- Swachh Bharat Abhiyan
- Jan-Dhan Yojana
- Deendayal Upadhyaya Gram Jyoti Yojana
- Kisan Fasal Bima Yojna
- Beti Padhao, Desh Badhao
- Ayushman Bharat Yojana,etc.

All these schemes intended to take administration to the doorstep of the common man by making the rural households, particularly the women, real beneficiaries of the Central Government schemes. The success of these schemes could be seen from the results of 2019 Lok Sabha elections where the voters across states – castes, classes, communities, gender and regions brought back the issues of development and governance to the centre stage. It was under the BJP led NDA Government characterising the current change with '*Sabka Saath, Sabka Vikas and Sabka Vishwas*'.

Chapter Practice

Objective Questions

• Multiple Choice Questions

1. Which of the following developments took place after 1980s in the country that had long lasting impact on politics?
(a) End of Congress System
(b) Mandal Commision, New Economic reforms
(c) Ayodhya dispute, assassination of Rajiv Gandhi
(d) All of the above

Ans. (d) Development in Indian politics after 1980s were
• End of Congress System
• Mandal Commission
• New Economic Reforms
• Ayodhya dispute
• Assassination of Rajiv Gandhi

2. Which year marked the end of what political scientist have called the 'Congress System'?
(a) 1984   (b) 1989
(c) 1991   (d) 1996

Ans. (b) The elections of 1989 marked the end of what political scientist have called the Congress system.

3. The Mandal Commission of 1990 declared that Other Backward Classes (OBCs) would get .... reservation in jobs, in Central Government services and public sector units.
(a) 18%   (b) 27%   (c) 35%   (d) 49%

Ans. (b) The Mandal Commision of 1990 declared that OBCs would get 27% reservation in jobs, in Central Government services and public sector units.

4. Which of the following party during its rule implemented one of the recommendations of the Mandal Commission in 1990?
(a) UPA   (b) NDA
(c) National Front   (d) Left Front

Ans. (c) The National Front Government in 1990 implemented one of the recommendations of the Mandal Commission.

5. Which of the following statement(s) is/are correct about new economic reforms?
(a) Rajiv Gandhi initiated Structural Adjustment Programme as the new economic reforms.
(b) The changes first became visible in 1991.
(c) The new economic reforms radically changed the direction of Indian economy after independence.
(d) All of the above

Ans. (d) Rajiv Gandhi initiated Structural Adjustment Programme or the new economic reforms. These changes first became visible in 1991 and radically changed the direction of Indian economy.

6. .... was a dispute between the Hindus and the Muslims over a mosque known as Babri Masjid.
(a) Ram Temple   (b) Ayodhya Dispute
(c) Babri Mosque   (d) Karseva Dispute

Ans. (b) Ayodhya dispute was a dispute between the Hindus and the Muslims over a mosque known as Babri Masjid.

7. What does Hindutva mean?
(a) It means Hinduness
(b) It was based on Indian nationhood
(c) It means everyone must accept India not only as their fatherland but also as their holyland
(d) All of the above

Ans. (d) Hindutva is the name by which the ideology of the Hindu right was founded in 1925. It is a predominant form of Hindu nationalism in India, popularised by VD Savarkar. It accepts India as their fatherland and holyland.

8. Prime Minister Rajiv Gandhi was assassinated during his election campaign tour in .... by a Sri Lankan Tamil associated to the LTTE.
(a) Andhra Pradesh   (b) Tamil Nadu
(c) Karnataka   (d) Kerala

Ans. (b) Prime Minister Rajiv Gandhi was assassinated during his election campaign tour in Tamil Nadu by a Sri Lankan Tamil associated to the LTTE in May 1991.

9. In the elections of 1991 Congress emerged as the single largest party. Following Rajiv Gandhi's death the party choose .... as the Prime Minister.
(a) PV Narsimha Rao   (b) Manmohan Singh
(c) VP Singh   (d) HD Deve Gowda

Ans. (a) PV Narsimha Rao was chosen as the Prime Minister after the death of Rajiv Gandhi.

10. Which of the following was elected as the Prime Minister during the coalition government formation in 1998 and 1999?

(a) PV Narasimha Rao   (b) Atal Bihari Vajpayee

(c) H D Deve Gowda   (d) J K Gujaral

Ans. (b) Atal Bihari Vajpayee was elected as the Prime Minister during the coalition government formation in 1998 and 1999.

11. In 1989, the National Front Government was supported by which two mutually opposed parties?

(a) Left Front and Congress

(b) Left Front and BJP

(c) BJP and Congress

(d) BSP and BJP

Ans. (b) In 1989, the National Front Government was supported by two mutually opposed parties i.e. Left Front and BJP.

12. Arrange the following in correct chronology.

(i) Formation of NDA Government

(ii) Appointment of Mandal Commission by Central Government

(iii) Janta Dal Formed

(iv) New Economic Reforms

Codes

(a) (ii), (iii), (iv) and (i)   (b) (i), (ii), (iii) and (iv)

(c) (iv), (ii), (iii) and (i)   (d) (ii), (iii), (i) and (iv)

Ans. (d) The correct chronology is

- Appointment of Mandal Commision by Central Government – 1979
- Janta Dal Formation – 1988
- Formation of NDA Government – 1998
- New Economic Reforms – 1991

13. Arrange the following in chronological order according to their period of prime ministership.

(i) IK Gujral

(ii) H D Deve Gowda

(iii) Narasimha Rao

(iv) Chandrashekhar

Codes

(a) (i), (ii), (iii) and (iv)

(b) (iv), (iii), (ii) and (i)

(c) (ii), (iv), (iii) and (i)

(d) (iv), (ii), (iii) and (i)

Ans. (b) The correct chronology is

- Chandrashekhar belonged to Samajwadi Party. He was the PM of India from 1927-2007.
- P V Narasimha Rao was the first PM from Soith India from 1921-2004.

- H D Deve Gowda belonged to Janata Dal Party. He was the PM of India from 1996-1997.
- I K Gujaral tenure as a PM was from 1997 to 1998.

14. Observe the picture given below and answer the following questions.

The picture depicts the Finance Minister Manmohan Singh, with Prime Minister .... in the initial phase of the 'New Economic Policy'.

(a) Indira Gandhi

(b) PV Narasimha Rao

(c) Rajiv Gandhi

(d) HD Deve Gowda

Ans. (b) Manmohan Singh, the then Finance Minister, with Prime Minister Narsimha Rao, in the initial phase of the 'New Economic Policy'.

15. Observe the picture given below and answer the following questions.

.... involves more compromises because different ideologies come together in it.

(a) One party   (b) A coalition

(c) Two-Party   (d) Socialist Party

Ans. (b) A coalition involves more compromises because different ideologies come together in it.

• Assertion-Reasoning MCQs

Directions (Q. Nos. 16-20) In the given questions, there are two statements marked as Assertion (A) and Reason (R). Read the statements and choose the correct code.

Codes
(a) Both A and R are true, but R is the correct explanation of A.
(b) Both A and R are true, but R is not the correct explanation of A.
(c) A is true, but R is false.
(d) A is false, but R is true.

16. Assertion (A) Elections in 1989 led to the defeat of the Congress party but did not result in a majority for any other party.

Reason (R) Though the Congress was the largest party in the Lok Sabha, it did not have a clear majority and therefore, it decided to sit in the opposition.

Ans. (a) Both A and R are true and R is the correct explanation of A. The defeat of Congress marked the end of Congress dominance over the Indian Party System. In 1989 elections, National Front formed a coalition government as it did not result in majority and Congress decided to sit in opposition.

17. Assertion (A) The BJP continued to consolidate its position in the elections of 1991 and 1996.

Reason (R) It emerged as the largest party in the 1996 election and was invited to form of the government.

Ans. (a) Both A and R are true and R is the correct explanation of A. The BJP emerged as the largest party in 1996 election but most other parties were opposed to its policies and therefore BJP government could not secure a majority in the Lok Sabha.

18. Assertion (A) A number of events culminated in the demolition of the disputed structure at Ayodhya (known as Babri Masjid) in December 1992.

Reason (R) The assassination of Rajiv Gandhi in May 1991 led to a change in leadership of the Congress party.

Ans. (b) Both A and R are true, but R is not the correct explanation of A. The demolition of disputed structure at Ayodhya symbolised and triggered various changes in the politics and intensified debates about Indian nationalism and secularism.

The assassination of Rajiv Gandhi led to change in leadership of Congress party. He was assassinated by a Sri Lankan Tamil linked to LTTE. Following Rajiv Gandhi's death, the party chose Narasimha Rao as the Prime Minister.

19. Assertion (A) The Mandal Commission was set up to investigate the extent of educational and social backwardness among various sections of Indian society and recommend ways of identifying these 'backward classes'.

Reason (R) The Commission gave its recommendations in 2000.

Ans. (c) A is true as the Mandal Commission was set up to investigate the extent of educational and social backwardness among various sections of Indian society. This commission is known after the name of its Chairperson, Bindeshwari Prasad Mandal.

R is false because the commission gave its recommendation in 1980. By then the Janta government had fallen.

20. Assertion (A) Rajiv Gandhi was assassinated by a Sri Lankan Tamil linked to the LTTE when he was on an election campaign tour in Tamil Nadu.

Reason (R) In the elections of 1991, Congress shrunk to the smallest party in the assembly.

Ans. (c) A is true as Rajiv Gandhi was assassinated by LTTE in May 1991 when he was an election campaign tour in Tamil Nadu.

R is false as in 1991 Congress emerged as the single largest party.

• Case Based MCQs

1. Read the following passage carefully and answer the questions that follow.

Way back in the late sixties, the dominance of the Congress party was challenged, but the Congress under the leadership of Indira Gandhi, managed to re-establish its predominant position in politics. The nineties as yet another challenge to the predominant position of the Congress. It did not, however, mean the emergence of any other single party to fill in its place.

Thus, began an era of multi-party system. To be sure, a large number of political parties always contested elections in our country. Our Parliament always had representatives from several political parties. What happened after 1989 was the emergence of several parties in such a way that one or two parties did not get most of the votes or seats. This also meant that no single party secured a clear majority of seats in any Lok Sabha election held since 1989. This development initiated an era of coalition governments at the Centre, in which regional parties played a crucial role in forming alliances.

(i) Multi-Party System refers to ....
(a) a system where only one party compete for power
(b) a system where two parties compete for power
(c) a system where many parties compete for power
(d) None of the above

Ans. (c) Multi-party system refers to a system where many parties compete for power.

(ii) Which kind of political scenario was witnessed after 1989?

(a) Era of coalitions

(b) Era of developments

(c) Era of regional parties

(d) Era of dominance

Ans. (a) The Era of Coalitions was witnessed after 1989. The term coalition has been derived from the Latin word meaning to go or grow together.

(iii) What is the reason behind the emergence of several parties?

(a) As no single party secured a clear majority of seats in the Lok Sabha elections.

(b) As the political scenario has changed completely.

(c) As the era of coalition began at the Centre level of government.

(d) None of the above

Ans. (a) The reason behind the emergence of several parties is that as no single party can secure a clear majority of seats in the Lok Sabha election so, many small parties come together with their terms and conditions to form a government and serve the interest of the people.

(iv) In the era of coalitions which type of parties played a crucial role in forming ruling alliances?

(a) National Parties　　　　(b) Unrecognised Parties

(c) Regional Parties　　　　(d) None of these

Ans. (c) In the era of Coalitions, recognised parties play a crucial role in forming a ruling alliance.

PART 2
Subjective Questions

• Short Answer Type Questions

1. Describe any two developments witnessed by India after 1990.　　　　　　　**[All India 2011]**

Ans. The two developments witnessed by India after 1990 are as follows

(i) **End of Congress System** This period witnessed the defeat of the Congress Party in the elections of 1989. The Party that had won 415 seats in the Lok Sabha in 1984 was reduced to only 197 seats in this election. The elections of 1989 marked the end of 'Congress System'. The Congress improved its performance and came back to power after the mid-term elections of 1991. The politics of this decade has clearly seen the impact of social change on political and electoral processes.

(ii) **New Economic Reforms** It was initiated by Rajiv Gandhi in 1991 which changed the direction of the Indian economy that was pursued since independence. The new economic reforms were widely criticised by various movements and

organisations. But various governments that came to power continued these policies. Reforms were evident in the form of additional sectors that were reserved for public investment was opened for private investment.

2. State any two important challenges faced by Indian politics during the 1990's.

Ans. Some of the important challenges faced by the Indian politics during the 1990's are discussed below

• **Mandal Issue** The rise of Mandal issue is one of the major challenges that Indian politics has faced during the 1990's. The new National Front Government in 1990 implemented the recommendation of the Mandal Commission. It held that jobs in Central Government should be reserved for the OBC's. This caused violent anti-Mandal protests in different parts of the country. The dispute was evident among the supporters and the opponents of OBC's reservations which came to be known as Mandal Issue. This issue helped in shaping the Indian politics since 1989.

• **Ayodhya Dispute** This dispute arose due to the demolition of Babri Masjid and rise of Hindutva Politics. A number of events resulted in the demolition of disputed structure known as Babri Masjid in December 1992. This event brought various changes in the politics of the country and intensified debates on the nature of Indian nationalism and secularism. These developments led to rise of BJP and politics of Hindutva.

3. In spite of the decline of Congress dominance, the Congress party continues to influence politics in the country. Do you agree? Give reasons.　　**[NCERT]**

Ans. The defeat of Congress party in 1989 election marked the end of Congress dominance in Indian party system. But the Congress continued to influence Indian politics because

• No other single party was able to fill the space left by Congress party.

• No single party was able to secure a clear majority in any Lok Sabha election since 1989.

• The emergence of powerful parties and movement that represented the Dalits and Backward Caste played important role in the formation of United Front under the support of Congress.

• Left Front started supporting Congress to curb the rise of Hindutva and communal politics of BJP.

Thus, despite the end of dominance, Congress party continued to influence the politics of the country.

4. "In the new era of coalition politics, political parties are not aligning or re-aligning on the basis of ideology." What arguments would you put forward to support or oppose this statement?　　**[NCERT]**

Ans. It is true that in the new era of coalition politics political parties are not aligning or re-aligning on the basis of ideology.

The statement is justified because political parties compete for political power ultimately. In the era of coalition politics, for them practical consideration rather than ideological consideration become driving factor for achieving political power. Some arguments to support this statement are as follows

- Coalition politics has shifted the focus from ideological differences to power sharing arrangements.
- Most parties of NDA did not agree with the *Hindutva* ideology of BJP, still they came together to form government and remained in power for full term.
- Dr Manmohan Singh's Government where the leftists supported the UPA (United Progressive Alliance), but in state both are opponents. The main interest was to keep out BJP from government. Same condition occurred in Bihar, when BJP and Janata Dal formed government to keep out RJD (Rashtriya Janata Dal).

5. "The regional parties have started playing an important role in the Indian politics." Comment.

Ans. India as democracy has the multi-party system which means there are several political parties competing for power. Apart from the national parties, each state has their own local political parties that rule and compete in their region.

Regional parties play the following roles in Indian politics

- In absence of clear majority, the largest party has to join hands with a regional party in order to form government. This is where the importance of the regional parties comes into play.
- Most of the regional parties have agenda furthering certain culture dominant within that state.
- The regional parties for their benefits divide the people of different states on the line of language, culture, traditions etc.
- Sometimes serious issues like India's foreign policy' are influenced and compromised by regional parties. This affects India's credibility in international politics.
- They also work as pressure groups in Indian politics.
- Sometimes regional parties influence the Central Government to divert more annual budget funds to their states at the expense of other states.

6. Analyse the changes that took place during a long phase of coalition politics in India since 1989.

[**CBSE 2020**]

Ans. Towards the end of 1980's, India witnessed a major change in the political field. These were

- In 1989 elections, the Congress won only 197 seats. Though Congress remains as a major party but it decided to sit in the opposition.
- The National Front, an alliance of Janta Dal and some other regional parties received external support from the BJP and the Left front. The National Front formed a coalition government. Thus, began the era of multi-party system in India.

- After 1989 till 2014, no single party secured a clear majority in any Lok Sabha elections.
- The Mandal issue started with the National Front government's decision to implement the recommendation of Mandal Commission in 1990. This issue started to play a crucial role in shaping Indian Politics.

7. Analyse the impact of political rise of Other Backward Classes in India. [**CBSE 2020**]

Ans. The impact of political rise of Other Backward Classes (OBC's) in India is

- When the support for the Congress among many sections of the backward castes had declined, this created a space for non-Congress parties to get the support of OBC's.
- Many of the constituents of the Janata Party like the Bhartiya Kranti Dal and Samyukta Socialist Party had a powerful rural base among some sections of the OBC.
- In the 1980's, the decisions of the National Front Government to implement the recommendations of the Mandal Commission further helped in shaping the politics of the OBC.
- 1980's saw the emergence of many parties like Bahujan Samaj Party (BSP) that sought better opportunities for OBC's in education, employment, adequate representation in administration.

8. What was the Mandal issue?

or Who was the Chairperson of Mandal Commission?

or Highlight any two recommendations of the Mandal Commission. [**Delhi 2013**]

Ans. Mandal issue in national politics followed the decision by the new National Front Government in 1990 to implement the recommendation of the Mandal Commission, that jobs in Central Government should be reserved for OBCs. This led to violence in many parts of the country especially in North India. This dispute between the supporters and opponents of OBC reservations was known as the Mandal issue and played an important role in shaping politics since 1989.

Bindeshwari Prasad Mandal was the Chairperson of Mandal Commission set-up in 1978 to investigate the extent of educational and social backwardness among various sections of society and recommended ways to identify these classes.

The two recommendations of the Mandal Commission are as follows

(i) It recommended reserving 27 percent of seat's in the educational institutions and government jobs for backward classes. It also made many other recommendations like land reforms, to improve the conditions of OBC's.

(ii) Welfare programmes specially meant for OBC's should be financed by the Government of India.

9. Why Mandal Commission was set up and what were its findings? Discuss its consequences after implementation.

Ans. It was setup to investigate the extent of educational and social backwardness among various sections of Indian society and recommended ways of identifying these backward classes. It was also expected to give its recommendations on the ways on which this backwardness could be ended.

One of its major findings was that the Commission found that these castes have very low presence in both educational institutions and in employment in public services.

Consequences of Implementing Mandal Commission

- This decision caused agitations and violent protests in many cities of North India.
- The decision was also challenged in the Supreme Court and came to be known as Indira Sawhney Case, after the name of the petitioners.
- In November 1992, the Supreme Court gave a ruling upholding the decision of the government.

10. Assess the impact of Coalition governments on the politics of India. **[CBSE 2020]**

Ans. The impacts of coalition governments on the politics of India are

(i) The parties in the coalition government believe in the same economic policy and think this would lead the country to prosperity and a status of economic power in the world.

(ii) All political parties now support reservation of seats for the backward classes in education and employment. Political parties in coalition government are willing to ensure that the OBC's get adequate share of power.

(iii) The distinction between State level and National level parties is becoming less important. State level parties are sharing power at the National level and have played a central role in the country's politics of last twenty years.

(iv) Coalition politics has shifted the focus of political parties from ideological differences to power sharing arrangements. Most parties in NDA do not agree with the Hindutva ideology of the BJP but they came together to form a government and remain in power for a full term.

11. Trace the emergence of BJP as a significant force in post-Emergency politics.

Ans. After Emergency, Bhartiya Jana Sangh had merged into the Janata Party. After the fall of the Janata Party and its break-up, the supporters of erstwhile Jana Sangh formed the Bharatiya Janata Party (BJP) in 1980. BJP adopted a broader political platform than that of the Jana Sangh. It

embraced 'Gandhian Socialism' as its ideology. But it did not get much success in the election of 1980 and 1984. After 1986, the party began to emphasise the Hindu nationalist element in its ideology.

Thus, BJP began to pursue the politics of 'Hindutva' and adopted the strategy of mobilising the Hindus. In 1996, BJP Minority Government was formed for a short period. In June 1996, BJP failed to get majority support in the vote of confidence and thus collapsed.

From March 1998 to October 1999, BJP and others formed alliances NDA (National Democratic Alliance) under the leadership of Atal Bihari Vajpayee and his government formed in 1999 completed its full term. Again in 2014 elections, BJP under the leadership of Modi came to power with landslide victory and also formed the governments almost in more than half of the states across India.

12. How can we say that NDA-III government schemes were successful?

Ans We can say that schemes of NDA-III government were successful due to the following reasons

- NDA-III government started several socio-economic welfare schemes to make development and governance accessible to the masses such as Pradhan Mantri Ujjwala Yojana, Jan Dhan Yojana, etc.
- All these schemes intended to make administration available at the doorstep of the common people by making the rural households, particularly women were, real beneficiaries of the Central Government schemes.
- The success of these schemes could be seen from the results of 2019 Lok Sabha elections, where the voters across states-castes, classes, communities, gender and regions brought back the issues of development and governance to the center stage under the BJP led NDA government.

13. Write a short note on United Progressive Alliance (UPA-I and II).

Ans. In the general elections of 2009, UPA won 262 seats, of which the Congress accounted for 206 seats. Manmohan Singh formed another UPA Coalition cabinet and was sworn in for the second term, becoming the first Prime Minister since Jawaharlal Nehru to do so after having served a full-five year term. The government made employment generation and social equity as the important features of its agenda.

Under UPA-II, women began occupying senior positions in State and Union Territories governments, notably in highly populated Tamil Nadu, Uttar Pradesh and West Bengal. It also works upon the issues of revitalising the agrarian economy, stepping up investment in agriculture, providing access to credit and improving the quality of rural infrastructure.

• Long Answer Type Questions

1. From 1989 to 2004, there have been nine coalition governments in India. Analyse the rise and fall of any two such coalition governments.

Ans. With the elections of 1989, a long phase of coalition politics began in India. Since then, there have been nine governments at the centre. All of them have either been coalition governments or minority governments supported by other parties which did not join the government. In this new phase, any government could be formed only with the participation of support of many regional parties. For example

(i) Nation Front Government in 1989.

(ii) The United Front Government in 1996 and 1997.

(iii) National Democratic Alliance (NDA), BJP led coalition in 1997, 1998, 1999.

(iv) United Progressive Alliance (UPA) in 2004.

United Front Government Some parties had Congress support and formed alliance in 1996 called United Front. In 1989, BJP and Left supported National Front. In 1989, BJP and Left wanted to keep the Congress out of power, hence, both supported National Front and later in 1996, Congress and Left both wanted to keep out BJP from the power. Therefore, both supported United Front in 1996.

United Progressive Alliance In 1996, BJP was invited to form the government, but most of the political parties, opposed its policies, consequently it could not secure a majority in the Lok Sabha.

In 2004 elections, the Congress party came to power with the new alliance known as United Progressive Alliance. This was a coalition in a big way. NDA was defeated and installation of another coalition led by Dr Manmohan Singh occurred. The UPA received support from DMK, PMK, AIADMK, RJD, NCP, TRS and Left from Andhra Pradesh, etc.

The 2004 election also saw the partial revival of Congress party as it increased its seats in comparision to 1996 elections.

2. "Coalition government is a bane or boon for democracy in India." Explain any three arguments in support of your answer. **[Delhi 2011]**

or Assess any three benefits of the coalition governments in India since 1989. **[Delhi 2010]**

Ans. Coalition government is a boon because

(i) **Participation of Regional Parties at National Level** State level parties played a crucial role in the country politics for last twenty years. Therefore, the differences between state level parties and central parties is decreasing day-by-day.

(ii) **Spirit of Adaptation** Coalition politics has shifted the focus of political parties from ideological distinctions to power sharing accommodation. We can see in the government of NDA that most of the parties did not agree with the ideology of Hindutva of BJP. However, they allied with BJP to form a government for a full term.

(iii) **Inclined Towards one Consensus** Various radical parties opposed the new economic policies, but some parties came to support new economic policies because they believed that these policies would lead the country towards prosperity and raise its status all over the world.

Coalition government is a bane for democracy in India because of three reasons

(i) **Unstable Government** The coalition government has its own interest and they fight for their own self interest. This leads to the breakup not only of various fronts but of governments as well.

(ii) **Political Opportunism** Government which is formed on the basis of coalition becomes selfish as opportunist power and unscrupulous politicians emphasise on their self interest only.

(iii) **Polarisation** The coalition governments are formed on the basis of polarisation of political forces. These are widely heterogeneous elements like CPI and BJP.

3. The Contemporary Party System is equated with the term 'BJP System' by the Social Scientists. With reference to the given statement discuss the factors responsible for it.

Ans. It is true that the Contemporary Party System has been equated with the term 'BJP System' by the Social Scientists. The factors responsible for this statement are discussed below

• The Bhartiya Janata Party led by PM Narendra Modi got an absolute majority in the Lok Sabha elections held in May 2014 and after nearly 30 years in the Indian politics; a strong government with an absolute majority was established at the Centre.

• The BJP-led Coalition NDA-III of 2014 was largely different from its predecessor coalition governments. The previous coalitions were led by one of the national parties, the NDA-III coalition was not only steered by the National Party, i.e. BJP rather it was also dominated by BJP with an absolute majority of its own in Lok Sabha. It was also called a surplus majority coalition.

• In that sense a major transformation could be seen in the nature of coalition politics which could be seen from one party led coalition to one party dominated coalition.

• The 2019 Lok Sabha elections, the 17th since Independence, once again brought back BJP led NDA (NDA-IV) to the centre of power by winning more than 350 seats out of 543. The BJP on its own won 303 seats in the Lok Sabha, the biggest number any single party has won in the lower house since 1984 when Congress swept the elections in the aftermath of Indira Gandhi's assassination.

• Case Based Questions

1. Read the passage and answer the questions below.

Party politics in India has confronted numerous challenges. Not only has the Congress system destroyed itself, but the fragmentation of the Congress coalition has triggered a new emphasis on self-representation which raises questions about the party system and its capacity to accommodate diverse interests, …… . An important test facing the polity is to evolve a party system or political parties that can effectively articulate and aggregate a variety of interests.
                                                            —**Zoya Hasan**

(i) Write a short note on what the author calls challenges of the party system in the light of what you have read in this chapter?

(ii) Given an example from this chapter of the lack of accommodation and aggregation mentioned in this passage.

(iii) Why is it necessary for parties to accommodate and aggregate variety of interests?

Ans. (i) Author calls the fragmentation of political parties on the basis of caste, creed, region, etc a challenge to party system in India. This has caused the trend of self-representation of one's own interest through formation of new party. This poses challenge to develop a party system or political parties that can effectively accommodate and articulate different interests of society.

(ii) Lack of accommodation and aggregation of the interests and concerns of Dalits led to the formation of BAMCEF (Backward and Minority Classes Employees Federation) under the leadership of Kanshi Ram to protect interests of Dalits.

(iii) It is necessary for parties to accommodate and aggregate the variety of interests to maintain the culture of India so that there should no space for separatist movements in India.

2. Read the passage given below carefully and answer the questions that follows.

The nineties also saw the emergence of powerful parties and movements that represented the Dalit and Backward Castes (Other Backward Classes or OBCs). Many of these parties represented powerful regional assertion as well. These parties played an important role in the United Front Government that came to power in 1996. The United Front was similar to the National Front of 1989 for it included Janata Dal and several regional parties. This time the BJP did not support the government. The United Front Government was supported by the Congress. This shows how unstable the political equations were. In 1989, both the Left and the BJP supported the National Front Government because they wanted to keep the Congress out of power. In 1996, the Left continued to support the non-Congress government but this time the Congress, supported it, as both the Congress and the Left wanted to keep the BJP out of power.

(i) What is the full form of OBC?

(ii) When was the United Front Government formed?

(iii) Name the two Prime Ministers from United Front Government.

Ans. (i) Other Backward Class (OBC) is a collective term used by the government to classify castes which are educationally or socially disadvantaged.

(ii) United Front Government was formed in India after 1996 elections. It was a coalition of 13 political parties.

(iii) HD Deve Gowda and I K Gujral were two Prime Ministers from United Front Government.

3. Observe the picture given below and answer the following questions.   **[Delhi 2016]**

(i) Identify any four national leaders from the above picture and mention the serial number of each.

(ii) Which was the most controversial issue of the period related to VP Singh as Prime Minister of India?

(iii) What was the position of the party led by leader No. 1 in the Lok Sabha elections of 1989?

Ans. (i) VP Singh, LK Advani, Chandrashekhar and Devi Lal are the four national leaders from the above picture.

(ii) Mandal issue was the most controversial issue of the period related to VP Singh as Prime Minister of India.

(iii) The party led by leader No. 1 got only 197 seats in the Lok Sabha election of 1989.

4. Observe the picture given below and answer the following questions. [All India 2016]

(i) Who was head of the government formed by the National Front in 1989?

(ii) Why was the government formed by him called a puppet government?

(iii) Identify the puppeters pulling the strings and the political parties they belong to.

Ans. (i) VP Singh was the head of the government formed by the National Front in 1989.

(ii) The government formed by him called a puppet government because

- The strings of this government were in the hands of other leaders.
- They were moving and controlling the government like a puppet by pulling the strings.

(iii) The puppeteers pulling the strings were Jyoti Basu and LK Advani.

(b) Jyoti Basu belong to Communist Party of India (Marxists) (CPM) and LK Advani belong to Bharatiya Janata Party (BJP).

Chapter Test

Objective Type Questions

1. Which of the following were the recommendations of the Mandal Commission?
   - (a) 27 percent seats to be reserved in educational institutions and government jobs for OBCs
   - (b) Land reform to improve the conditions of OBCs
   - (c) Commission made recommendation in economic and occupational structures
   - (d) All of the above

2. Which of the following aspects is/are incorrect about UPA?
   - (a) In General Elections of 2009, UPA won 262 seats, of which Congress accounted for 206 seats.
   - (b) UPA government made employment generation and social equity as the important features of its agenda.
   - (c) Under UPA-II, women began occupying senior positions in State and Union Territories.
   - (d) Its main goal is based on 'Sabka Saath, Sabka Vikas'.

3. How many seats were gained by BJP in the Lower House on its own in the 2019 Lok Sabha Elections?
   - (a) 262
   - (b) 292
   - (c) 302
   - (d) 303

4. Godhra incident is associated with which place?
   - (a) Mumbai
   - (b) Uttar Pradesh
   - (c) Gujarat
   - (d) Bihar

5. BJP led coalition of 2014 was also called as ....
   - (a) Majority Coalition
   - (b) Surplus Majority Coalition
   - (c) Clear Majority Coalition
   - (d) Democratic Coalition

Short Answer Type Questions

1. When and why was the first coalition government formed?
2. Explain the role of regional parties in coalition politics.
3. What is Mandal Commission?
4. Which coalition came to power in 2004? Name its supporting parties.
5. Give any two arguments in favour of reservation for the SCs, STs and OBCs in higher education institutions in India.

Long Answer Type Questions

1. Explain the features of coalition politics.
2. Is there any relevance of Mandal Commission? Discuss.
3. Explain any three elements of consensus which have emerged among most political parties.
4. Analyse the changes that took place during a long phase of coalition politics in India since 1989.

Answers

1. *(d)* 2. *(d)* 3. *(d)* 4. *(c)* 5. *(c)*

Practice Paper 1*
(Solved)

General Instructions

- **Time :** 2 Hours
- **Max. Marks :** 40

1. There are 9 questions in the question paper. All questions are compulsory.
2. Question no. 1 is a Case Based Question, which has five MCQs. Each question carries 1 mark.
3. Question no. 2-6 are Short Type Questions. Each question carries 3 marks.
4. Question no. 7-9 are Long Answer Type Questions. Each question carries 5 marks.
5. There is no overall choice. However, internal choice have been provided in some questions. Students have to attempt only on of the alternatives in such questions

** As exact Blue-print and Pattern for CBSE Term II exams is not released yet. So the pattern of this paper is designed by the author on the basis of trend of past CBSE Papers. Students are advised not to consider the pattern of this paper as official. It is just for practice purpose.*

Case Based MCQs

1. Read the given passage and answer the following questions.

The Chinese leadership took major policy decisions in the 1970s. China ended its political and economic isolation with the establishment of relations with the United States in 1972. Premier Zhou Enlai proposed the 'four modernisations'(agriculture, industry, science and technology and military) in 1973. By 1978, the then leader Deng Xiaoping announced the 'open door' policy and economic reforms in China. The policy was to generate higher productivity by investments of capital and technology from abroad. China followed its own path in introducing a market economy. The Chinese did not go for 'shock therapy' but opened their economy step by step. The privatisation of agriculture in 1982 was followed by the privatisation of industry in 1998. Trade barriers were eliminated only in Special Economic Zones (SEZs) where foreign investors could set up enterprises. In China, the state played and continues to play a central role in setting up a market economy. $(1 \times 5 = 5)$

(i) Which among the following does not include in the four modernisation theory of Premier Zhou Enlai?
    (a) Agriculture   (b) Investment   (c) Industry   (d) Military

(ii) Who among the following announced the ' Open Door Policy'?
    (a) Premier Zhou Enlai   (b) Deng Xiaoping   (c) Xi Jinping   (d) Both (b) and (c)

(iii) China introduce its own path in introducing a ....
    (a) Market economy   (b) Mixed economy   (c) Socialist economy   (d) None of these

(iv) Trade barriers were eliminated in which of the following sector?
    (a) Inclusive zone   (b) Science and technology
    (c) Domestic market   (d) Special Economic Zone

(v) Which of the following country is not a member of ASEAN?
    (a) Philippines   (b) Mauritius   (c) Thailand   (d) Singapore

Short Answer Type Questions

1. Evaluate any major factors responsible for making the European Union a political force from; being an economic force. 　　3 Marks

Or How far is it correct to describe ASEAN as an alternative Centre of power in the world?

2. Explain any four causes of ethnic conflict in Sri Lanka. 　　3 Marks

Or Explain any two reasons for the popular struggle in East Pakistan (now Bangladesh) against West Pakistan during 1971.

3. How are the external powers influencing bilateral relations in South Asia? Take any one example to illustrate your point. 　　3 Marks

4. The Shah Commission was appointed in 1977 by the Janata Party Government. Why was it appointed and what were its findings? 　　3 Marks

Or What reasons, do you think, were responsible for the declaration of emergency in 1975? Examine any two reasons.

5. Describe the era of multi-party system in India after 1989. 　　3 Marks

Long Answer Type Questions

1. What is meant by globalisation? List any two forms of resistance to globalisation. 　　5 Marks

Or What is worldwide interconnectedness? What are its components?

2. Analyse the reasons for the dominance of Congress Party in the first three general elections. 　　5 Marks

Or Why were the general elections of 1967 called as the political earthquake for Congress? Examine any four reasons.

3. Why is Emergency considered to be one of the most controversial episodes in Indian politics? Analyse any three reasons. 　　5 Marks

Or Assess any three happenings which were responsible for the downfall of the Congress Party in the 1977 elections.

4. When and why did a long phase of coalition politics begin in India? 　　5 Marks

Answers

Case Based MCQs

1. (i) (b),　(ii) (b),　(iii) (a),　(iv) (d),　(v) (b)

Short Answer Type Questions

1. European Union (EU) is a very strong regional organisation of European countries. It plays an important role in world politics. European Union is also called European Common Market or European Common Community. Factors responsible for making the European Union a political force from being an economic force are

- The two World Wars within a very short duration inflicted very heavy losses upon European countries. During six years of the Second World War, European countries suffered heavy economic, material and manpower losses. The Second World War shattered many of the assumptions and structures on which the European states had based their relations.

- After the Second World War majority of the European leaders were convinced that their relations should be reconstructed. They were compelled to find out solutions from the European perspective and ultimately formed an organisation known as the European Union.

- European Union is a very strong organisation of European countries. European Union is also called the European Common Market or European Common Community. The European Union is the world's largest economy with a GDP of more than $12 trillion in 2005. Within a short period of time, it became a very powerful economic and political organisation. It has its own parliament, own flag, anthem and its own currency. The E.U. also exercises political and diplomatic influence.

Or

ASEAN still remain principally an economic association. ASEAN was established in 1967 by five countries of this region. This region is much smaller than other associations like EU, the US and Japan. The main objective of ASEAN was to accelerate economic growth. ASEAN is rapidly growing into a very important regional organisation. It is the basis of creating a common market and production within the region and boost social and economic development in the region.

It has created a Free-Trade Area for investment, labour and services. Its vision 2020 has defined an outward-looking role for ASEAN in the international community. In its vision 2020 ASEAN has hoped that it will become very strong in an economy that it will be able to play an important role in international affairs.

2. The four causes of ethnic conflict were

   (i) The bone of contention was the region of Ceylon which was represented by the majority Sinhala group. They opposed the migration and settlements of Tamilians from India in their region.

   (ii) According to the group Sri Lanka was only for Sinhala people and not for Tamils. This attitude of Sinhala people led to the establishment of Liberation Tigers of Tamil Eelam (LTTE), a militant organisation, which desired for a separate country.

   (iii) There was a pressure on the Government of India by the Tamils of Indian origin to intervene in the matter. Hence, the Government of India tried to negotiate with the Government of Sri Lanka on Tamil question. But direct involvement was in the year 1987. India conceded to sent troops to Sri Lanka for the preservation of relations between Tamils and Sri Lanka Government. Eventually, the Indian troops got into a fight with LTTE.

   (iv) The presence of Indian troops was not liked by many Sri Lankans and hence in 1989, the Indian Peace Keeping Force (IPKF) pulled out of Sri Lanka without attaining its objective.

Or The two reasons for the popular struggle in East Pakistan (now Bangladesh) against West Pakistan during 1971 are following

   (i) After Independence of both India and Pakistan, Bangladesh was a part of Pakistan and was called East Pakistan. The Government of Pakistan imposed Urdu language forcefully on East Pakistan's people.

   (ii) The West Pakistan imposed its own culture and it led to unfair treatment on Bengali culture and language. The people of East Pakistan also wanted fair representation in the administration and political power.

3. The external powers are influencing bilateral relations in South Asia like. China and United States remain a key player in South Asian politics. America has been influencing the bilateral relations in South Asia since the end of the Cold War in the following ways

   • The United States has worked as a moderator in Indo-Pakistan relations.

   • Economic reforms and liberal economic politics in both the countries have increased the American participation.

   • The South Asian diaspora are working in USA and this gives America added stake in the future of regional security and peace.

4. In May 1977, the Janata Party Government appointed Shah Commission of inquiry headed by Justice JC Shah, retired Chief Justice of the Supreme Court of India. It was appointed to look into the misuse of authority by government and conduct of unethical practices like demolition of Jhuggis, forced sterilisation, etc which were conducted in the wake of Emergency. The commission gathered various evidences and recorded witnesses to give testimonies. The findings of Shah Commission were

   • It found out that Preventive Detention was widely used by the government. Around one lakh eleven thousand arbitrary arrests were made by the government.

   • Newspapers were asked to get permission before publishing of any matter. In Delhi, Lieutenant Governor ordered General Manager of Delhi Power Supply to cut off the power supply of news press till they establish censorship apparatus.

Or The circumstances which led to the proclamation of emergency were

   (i) Bihar and Gujarat's movement created an unrest in the country. Students were protesting against the price rise and against the established government in these states. Congress as ruling party failed to handle these protests. Leadership by influencial leaders further gave them a momentum against government.

   (ii) Increases in Naxalite activities against government and violent nature troubled the government. Naxalite had an anti government view. Even harsh measures by government could not stop them.

   (iii) Declaration of Indira Gandhi's 1971 election invalid was a last straw. Jai Prakash Narayan organised a massive demonstration demanding her resignation. The situation was tense and emergency was declared on 25th June, 1975.

   (iv) Call of complete revolution by Jai Prakash Narayan and unexpected people movement in Delhi.

   (v) Jai Prakash Narayan announced a nationwide satyagraha for resignation and asked the army, the police and government employees not to obey 'illegal and immoral orders'.

5. Elections in 1989 led to the defeat of the Congress party but did not result in a majority for any other party. Though Congress was the largest party in the Lok Sabha, it did not have a clear majority.

The defeat of the Congress party marked the end of Congress dominance over the Indian party system. Way back in the late sixties, the dominance of the Congress party was challenged; but the Congress under the leadership of Indira Gandhi managed to re-establish its predominant position in politics. The nineties saw yet another challenge to the predominant position of the Congress. It did not, however, mean the emergence of any other single party to fill in its place. Thus, began an era of a multi-party system.

To be sure, a large number of political parties always contested elections in our country. Our Parliament always had representatives from several political parties. What happened after 1989 was the emergence of several parties in such a way that one or two parties did not get most of the votes of seats. This also meant that no single party secured a clear majority of seats in any Lok Sabha election held since 1989. This development initiated an era of coalition governments at the Centre, in which regional parties played a crucial role in forming ruling alliances.

The nineties also saw the emergence of powerful parties and movements that represented the Dalit and backward castes (Other Backward Classes or OBC). Many of these parties represented powerful regional assertion as well.

Long Answer Type Questions

1. Globalisation means the flows of ideas, capital, commodities and people across different parts of the world. It is a multidimensional concept. It has political, economic and cultural manifestations and these must be adequately distinguished. The effect of globalisation is uneven as it is not based on general conclusions within different societies. Every society is impacted in a different manner like some societies are impacted more than others.

The four reasons due to which globalisation is resisted are

- Leftist parties argue that contemporary globalisation represents a global capitalism that makes the rich richer and the poor poorer.
- Weakening of the state leads to a reduction in the capacity of the state to protect the interest of its poor.
- Rightist parties express anxiety over the political economic and cultural effects.
- The cultural globalisation would harm age old values of people while harming their traditional culture.

Or Globalisation is defined as worldwide interconnectedness. Globalisation fundamentally means the flow of ideas, capital, commodities and people across different parts of the world. The crucial element is the 'worldwide interconnectedness', that is created and sustained as a consequence of these constant flows. It is a multi-dimensional concept as it has political, economic and cultural manifestations and these must be adequately distinguished. The impact of globalisation is vastly uneven because it affects some societies more than others and some parts of some societies more than others. The major components of worldwide interconnectedness i.e. globalisation are

Technological Advancement Technology It remains an important factor with regard to globalisatioin. The technological inventions such as telegraph, telephone and the microchip has revolutionised communication between various global factors. Thus, technological advancements have been most significant component of worldwide interconnectedness.

Free Flow of Capital and Investment It has also been the key component of rising worldwide interconnectedness. Flow of FDI across the world has transform the world into a interconnected global market.

Migration and Movement of People It has also been responsible for growing worldwide interconnectedness. Technological advancement has reduced the physical distances and increased the migration and movement of people from one country to another.

Sharing of Ideas and Knowledge It has also been responsible for increasing interconnectedness. With technological advancement, ideas and knowledge are rapidly moving from one part to another parts of world.

2. The Congress Party succeed in maintaining its dominance till 1967 due to following reasons

  (i) The roots of this extraordinary success of the Congress Party go back to the legacy of the freedom struggle. Congress was seen as inheritor of the national movement. Many leaders who were in forefront of the struggle were now contesting elections as Congress candidates.

  (ii) The Congress Party was supported by elites, educated business classes and middle classes people. It also got support from peasants because of its socialist nature.

  (iii) It had many popular faces like Jawaharlal Nehru, C Rajagopalachari, Vallabhbhai Patel, etc. Moreover, Jawaharlal Nehru was charismatic and very popular leader.

  (iv) Congress worked at upper level as well as at grassroot level. Congress was popularised due to the participation in civil disobedience movement.

  (v) During period of Nehruji, Congress attained mass popularity, but the powerful narrow elite of Congress confined to benefit from the low level of political consciousness of the electorate.

  (vi) The traditional loyalities made Congress a one-party dominance.

Or The general elections of 1967 called as the political earthquake for Congress party. The results of 1967 elections jolted the Congress at both the national and state level. Congress managed to get majority in the Lok Sabha but with its lowest tally of seats and share of votes since 1952. The reasons behind this were

  (i) The Fourth General Election held in 1967 was the first election to be held without Jawaharlal Nehru.

  (ii) Congress was dominant party before 1967, but scenario was likely to change after 1967's election. Several non-Congress parties joined together to bring Congress down. They realised that their disintegration kept Congress in power. So, they joined to form a big alliance called Samyukt Vidhayak Dal.

(iii) Congress still managed to win in Lok Sabha election, but with the poorest performance ever. Congress lost in many states and influential leaders of Congress lost their positions.

(iv) Many Congress leaders left the party in order to join the other party. Local politics gained momentum. Defection and coalition played an important role and new elements were in the scene of electoral politics.

3. Emergency is one of the most controversial episodes in Indian politics. Most of promises by the government remained unfulfilled that were simply meant to divert attention from the excesses that were taking place. They question the use of Preventive Detention on such a large scale. Many prominent political leaders were arrested. In all, 676 opposition leaders were arrested. he Shah Commission estimated that nearly one lakh eleven thousand people were arrested under Preventive Detention laws. Severe restrictions were put on the press, sometimes without proper legal sanctions. The Shah Commission report mentions that the General Manager of the Delhi Power Supply Corporation Received verbal orders from the office of the Lt. Governor of Delhi to cut electricity of all newspaper presses at 2:00 am on 26th June, 1975.

Electricity was restored two to three days later after the censorship apparatus had been set-up. Democracy remained suspended during Emergency. Democratic way of expression of feeling, anger, dissatisfaction, etc through protest, agitation, etc were crushed bitterly by government. And Emergency was imposed by the Government despite having majority to crush the democratic movement against the ruling party. Government suspended the freedom of press, newspapers were asked to take permission before publishing any matter. Fundamental Rights of citizens were suspended including the right to move to the court for restoring Fundamental Rights.

Or

Three happenings which were responsible for the downfall of the Congress Party in the 1977 elections were

(i) The major opposition parties had already come closer in the pre-Emergency period. They came together on the eve of the elections and formed a new party known as the Janata Party.

(ii) Some leaders of the Congress who were opposed to the Emergency also joined this new party. Some other Congress leaders also came out and formed a separate party under the leadership of Jagjivan Ram.

(iii) The Janata Party's campaign focussed on the non-democratic character of the rule and on the various excesses that took place during the Emergency. The opposition to Emergency could keep the Janata Party together only for a while because the party lacked direction, leadership and a common programme.

4. The long phase of coalition politics began in India in 1989 because

(i) No political party able to get majority despite of Congress being the largest party in Lok Sabha elections. So in 1977, the Janata party formed government with the support of many non-Congress parties.

(ii) United Front Government was formed under Prime Ministership of Chandra Shekhar, then under HD Deve Gowda and finally IK Gujral with the outside support of BJP and leftists.

(iii) In 1999 to 2004, NDA run the government under Prime Ministership of Atal Bihari Vajpayee. lt was the first coalition government which completed its full term.

(iv) In 2004 to 2014, UPA run the government under Dr. Manmohan Singh, it is another coalition government which run for two terms. Thus, coalition governments were not stable in earlier times, but after 1999 they emerged as stable governments.

Practice Paper 2*
(Unsolved)

General Instructions

- **Time :** 2 Hours
- **Max. Marks :** 40

1. There are 9 questions in the question paper. All questions are compulsory.
2. Question no. 1 is a Case Based Question, which has five MCQs. Each question carries 1 mark.
3. Question no. 2-6 are Short Type Questions. Each question carries 3 marks.
4. Question no. 7-9 are Long Answer Type Questions. Each question carries 5 marks.
5. There is no overall choice. However, internal choice have been provided in some questions. Students have to attempt only on of the alternatives in such questions

__ As exact Blue-print and Pattern for CBSE Term II exams is not released yet. So the pattern of this paper is designed by the author on the basis of trend of past CBSE Papers. Students are advised not to consider the pattern of this paper as official. It is just for practice purpose.__*

Case Based MCQs

1. Study the following and answer the questions.

The lack of genuine international support for democratic rule in Pakistan has further encouraged the military to continue its dominance. The United States and other Western countries have encouraged the military's authoritarian rule in the past, for their own reasons. Given their fear of the threat of what they call 'global Islamic Terrorism' and the apprehension that Pakistan's nuclear arsenal might fall into the hands of these terrorist groups, the military regime in Pakistan has been seen as the protector of Western interests in West Asia and South Asia.

$(1 \times 5 = 5)$

(i) What is the hurdle of democracy in Pakistan?
 (a) It has no experience of any regular democracy
 (b) Democracy did not get any solid footing and development
 (c) Due to circumstances, military rule is regarded as the best option in Pakistan
 (d) All of the above

(ii) What did the Western countries encourage the military to continue its dominance in Pakistan?
 (a) As they fear that Global Islamic Terrorism may become active
 (b) Military regime in Pakistan has been the protector of the Western Interest in West Asia and South Asia
 (c) As it was benefitting the Western countries
 (d) Both (a) and (b)

(iii) Which among the following initiative must be taken by the citizens of Pakistan in establishing democracy?
 (a) They must play an active role in establishing democracy
 (b) The citizen of Pakistan should use their courage and intellect for fighting for democracy
 (c) Military rule must be discouraged and benefits of democracy must be encouraged
 (d) Both (a) and (b)

(iv) Military rule is regarded as the best option in Pakistan because......
    (a) democracy was never developed and encouraged in Pakistan
    (b) due to strong military influence on the citizens
    (c) due to fear and enmity among the citizens
    (d) None of the above

(v) Which factors contributed to Pakistan's failure in building a stable democracy?
    (a) Dominance of democracy   (b) Dominance of clergy
    (c) Dominance of land owning aristocracy   (d) All of these

Short Answer Type Questions

1. Explain any three reasons for resistance to globalisation.

Or Explain any two major causes of globalisation.   3 Marks

2. Distinguish between cultural homogenisation and cultural heterogenisation.

Or How has technology contributed to globalisation? Explain.   3 Marks

3. Describe any four features of the Congress Party.

Or Highlight two features of the ideology of Bhartiya Jana Sangh.   3 Marks

4. Highlight any two constitutional issues between the Parliament and the Judiciary during the 1970s.   3 Marks

5. In spite of the decline of Congress dominance, the Congress party continues to influence politics in the country. Do you agree? Give reasons.   3 Marks

Long Answer Type Questions

1. What makes European Union a highly influential regional organisation?

Or How did the European countries resolve their post-Second World War problem? Briefly outline the attempts that led to the formation of the European Union.   5 Marks

2. What are the economic implications of globalisation? How has globalisation impacted on India with regard to this particular dimension?   5 Marks

Or How has globalisation impacted India and how is India impacting globalisation?

3. Explain the major outcome of 1977 Lok Sabha elections.   5 Marks

4. From 1989 to 2004, there have been nine coalition governments in India. Analyse the rise and fall of any two such coalition governments.   5 Marks

Practice Paper 3*
(Unsolved)

General Instructions

- **Time :** 2 Hours
- **Max. Marks :** 40

1. There are 9 questions in the question paper. All questions are compulsory.
2. Question no. 1 is a Case Based Question, which has five MCQs. Each question carries 1 mark.
3. Question no. 2-6 are Short Type Questions. Each question carries 3 marks.
4. Question no. 7-9 are Long Answer Type Questions. Each question carries 5 marks.
5. There is no overall choice. However, internal choice have been provided in some questions.
   Students have to attempt only on of the alternatives in such questions

** As exact Blue-print and Pattern for CBSE Term II exams is not released yet. So the pattern of this paper is designed by the author on the basis of trend of past CBSE Papers. Students are advised not to consider the pattern of this paper as official. It is just for practice purpose.*

Case Based MCQs

1. Read the following passage carefully and answer the questions that follow.

Way back in the late sixties, the dominance of the Congress party was challenged, but the Congress under the leadership of Indira Gandhi, managed to re-establish its predominant position in politics. The nineties as yet another challenge to the predominant position of the Congress. It did not, however, mean the emergence of any other single party to fill in its place. Thus, began an era of multi-party system. To be sure, a large number of political parties always contested elections in our country. Our Parliament always had representatives from several political parties. What happened after 1989 was the emergence of several parties in such a way that one or two parties did not get most of the votes or seats. This also meant that no single party secured a clear majority of seats in any Lok Sabha election held since 1989. This development initiated an era of coalition governments at the Centre, in which regional parties played a crucial role in forming alliances.

(i) Multi-Party System refers to ....
   (a) a system where only one party compete for power.
   (b) a system where two parties compete for power.
   (c) a system where many parties compete for power.
   (d) None of the above

(ii) Which kind of political scenario was witnessed after 1989?
   (a) Era of coalitions
   (b) Era of developments
   (c) Era of regional parties
   (d) Era of dominance

(iii) What is the reason behind the emergence of several parties?
    (a) As no single party secured a clear majority of seats in the Lok Sabha elections.
    (b) As the political scenario has changed completely.
    (c) As the era of coalition began at the Central level of government.
    (d) None of the above

(iv) In the era of coalitions which type of parties played a crucial role in forming ruling alliances?
    (a) National Parties   (b) Unrecognised Parties
    (c) Regional Parties   (d) None of these

(v) Which of the following was elected as the Prime Minister during the coalition government formation in 1998 and 1999?
    (a) PV Narasimha Rao   (b) Atal Bihari Vajpayee
    (c) HD Deve Gowda   (d) JK Gujaral

Short Answer Type Questions

1. Discuss the relations of India and Maldives and its importance for India.   3 Marks

Or Discuss the relations of India and Sri Lanka in detail.

2. "Globalisation has shifted power from nation-states to global consumers." Justify the statement.   3 Marks

Or Describe effects of globalisation on the economy of a country.

3. Examine the factors which helped VV Giri to become the President of India.   3 Marks

Or The phrase 'Aaya Ram Gaya Ram' signifies which concept? Explain its impact on the Indian political system.

4. How did the Emergency of 1975 benefit the Indian democratic set-up?   3 Marks

5. Write a short note on Jayaprakash Narayan.   3 Marks

Long Answer Type Questions

1. Define ASEAN. What steps should be taken to strengthen it?   5 Marks

Or Explain any six reasons for the rise of the Chinese economy.

2. Describe India's relationship with Pakistan in context of recent developments.   5 Marks

Or What are the contentious issues between India and Bangladesh?

3. Describe any three effects of globalisation on the economy of a country.   5 Marks

Or "Globalsation has shifted power from nation-states to global consumers." Justify the statement.

4. How did the fourth general elections (1967) in India change the dynamics of Indian politics?   5 Marks

Printed by Libri Plureos GmbH in Hamburg,
Germany